database
marketing

database
marketing

know what your
customer wants

IAN LINTON

Pitman Publishing would like to thank The Business Database and its clients for providing advice and case studies, and for the invaluable contribution they have made to this book.

PITMAN PUBLISHING
128 Long Acre, London WC2E 9AN

A Division of Pearson Professional Limited

First published in Great Britain 1995

© Pearson Professional Limited 1995

British Library Cataloguing in Publication Data
A CIP catalogue record for this book can be obtained from the British Library.

ISBN 0 273 61179 8

10 9 8 7 6 5 4

Typeset by Northern Phototypesetting Co Ltd, Bolton
Printed and bound in Great Britain by Bell and Bain Ltd, Glasgow

The Publishers' policy is to use paper manufactured from sustainable forests.

contents

1

the business benefits of database marketing

This chapter introduces the concept of database marketing and explains how it can be used to achieve significant business benefits by supporting and improving performance across the whole spectrum of sales and marketing techniques.

what is database marketing?

Database marketing is not a substitute for traditional marketing activities - it is a way of improving the performance of those activities through the effective use of customer information. Collecting and using data on your customers and your markets helps you to gain a better understanding of the market so that you can utilize sales and marketing techniques in a more precise, cost-effective way. The box below shows how data gathered from one marketing campaign can be used to support a range of other activities.

Data supports sales and marketing activities

Data from response to an advertisement generates:

- Prospect list for the telemarketing team to qualify leads.
- Quality leads for salesforce contact.
- Mailing lists for regular customer contact.
- List for developing targeted sales promotion offers.
- Basis for evaluating the effectiveness of different advertising media.
- Prospect information for tracking subsequent purchases.
- Basis for evaluating the effectiveness of conversion strategies.

Database marketing provides you with a detailed picture of the market and allows you to answer questions such as:

- Who are our most important customers?
- How many are there?
- What characteristics do they have?
- What other prospects have similar characteristics?
- Are we generating the maximum amount of business from each customer?
- Are we maximizing the business opportunities from each customer contact?

- Do we really know what our customers want?

- What factors and marketing activities affect their buying behaviour?

- Can we identify every product our customers might use?

- Do we know every transaction they might want to make?

- Is information available to everyone who might need it?

- Is our organization giving the right information to the marketplace?

- What would happen if we varied our marketing spend or used different marketing channels?

Armed with a customer and market profile like this, the approach to sales and marketing becomes more scientific. You can measure the effectiveness of campaigns, compare the results of different approaches or offers and monitor progress towards your key objectives.

Database marketing can benefit your business by improving marketing precision and improving the relationships between you and your most important customers. The long-term customer relationships at the heart of database marketing enable you to plan the future development of your business with greater confidence and contribute to an overall reduction of your sales and marketing costs.

WATCH OUT!

Database marketing does not improve all aspects of marketing by itself. It underpins the sales and marketing skills you have and supports the campaigns you run. However, it is no substitute for employing good sales and marketing people and running well-planned campaigns. Nor will database marketing produce improvements if the data is poor.

what does database marketing involve?

Database marketing uses computer systems and data to provide information for planning and controlling sales and marketing activities. The computer systems provide the ability to store and manipulate large amounts of data from diverse sources and present information in a convenient, accessible and useful format.

Data can come from a variety of internal and external sources and can be constantly updated, expanded and refined to provide a precise, up-to-date view of markets and individual customers. Software tools are available to analyze the data and provide information in a way that improves decision-making and response to business opportunities.

key aspects of database marketing

Database techniques allow you to improve performance in a number of key areas:

● Understanding customers.

● Managing customer service.

● Understanding the market.

● Understanding competitors.

● Managing sales operations.

● Managing marketing campaigns.

● Communicating with customers.

UNDERSTANDING CUSTOMERS The customer knowledge and feedback developed through database marketing helps you to develop an effective strategy for long-term customer retention. Long-term customers add vital stability to a company. Most companies have a base of regular customers, but few know why those customers keep coming back. Quality, price, delivery, convenience; these are some of the factors that could explain why a customer continues to buy from your company but, unless you understand the factors behind your success, you cannot plan a customer retention strategy for the future. You need to understand your customers' business, their plans, their key concerns and their views of you as a supplier, and you need to be certain that you can continue to provide them with the service they need. The discipline of building and using a database helps you concentrate on these important issues.

You may already have the nucleus of a customer database within your company in the form of sales records, accounts records, customer enquiries, exhibition leads and complaints. However, unless this information is integrated, you will not be able to get a single view of the customer as a basis for marketing planning and action.

By bringing this information together in a single database, you can get a comprehensive view of individual customers and customer groups and assess the effect of different marketing activities on their purchasing behaviour. This is the kind of customer and market profile you can develop using database techniques:

● Which market sectors do customers and prospects fit into?

● How many are in each sector?

● What products do they buy?

● What other products could be offered to these sectors?

● Which sectors offer the best growth opportunities?

● Which are the most valuable sectors?

● Who are the key customers in each sector?

● How profitable are the key customers?

● What is the cost of each customer?

Having this customer profile on a single database is a starting point. You can then use it to provide sales and marketing people with information they need to put campaigns and programmes into action.

FAST TRACK

○ *Make sure the salesforce have an up-to-date profile of customers and prospects.*

○ *Refine your sales structure to reflect the key sectors.*

○ *Use the customer profile to plan communications strategies and select media that concentrate on key sectors.*

MANAGING CUSTOMER SERVICE

Understanding your customers is the first step to developing positive, long-term relationships with them. The customer information you hold on your database can be used in several important ways:

● To improve customer handling by making information available to staff responsible for sales, enquiries, helplines, order processing, complaints, service or other customer-facing activities.

- To improve understanding of the customer's purchasing life cycle.

- To identify opportunities to offer customers a range of other products or services tailored to their individual needs. Taken to its logical conclusion, this could enable you to deal with customers as individuals on a one-to-one basis - a very powerful form of niche marketing.

Database marketing techniques provide a detailed understanding of your customers' overall purchasing patterns and that may enable you to influence the frequency of purchase cycles through the higher levels contact and the introduction of customer support services. Every product goes through a life cycle and this can give important clues to the additional products and services a customer might need. Customers' needs change as they progress through the life cycle. They may need help in introducing a product, making the best use of it or preparing for change.

The process of life cycle analysis can be used in any purchase situation where frequency of contact is important. Analyzing the database can help to identify purchasing patterns throughout the life cycle. Database marketing can shorten that cycle by focusing on the customer's needs throughout the "life cycle" of a product.

Database marketing not only influences purchasing frequency, it can encourage repeat purchase and provide a valuable opportunity for selling related products and services. For example, companies which market capital goods have an immediate opportunity to sell parts, service and accessories over an extended period, as well as a wide range of customer support services. Database marketing offers an opportunity to build "customers for life".

FAST TRACK

○ *Ensure that all customer-facing staff have access to customer information on the database.*

○ *Use the information as the basis for planning individual "customer strategies".*

Your company may already carry out market research regularly, or on an ad-hoc basis. By integrating market research findings with the other information on your database, you can build a more sophisticated view of the marketplace as a basis for future segmentation strategies.

These are some of the key questions you can address through the database:

- What are the key market sectors for different products in our portfolio?

- Which are the growth sectors and which are static or declining?

- What share of the market do we and our competitors hold?

- Which sectors are the most profitable?

- Which sectors are "crowded" and which have not been exploited?

- What are the characteristics of our main market sectors?

- Do any other sectors share similar characteristics?

This information can help you to decide where to allocate your sales and marketing resources to achieve the most effective return. It can also help you to identify new market sectors that offer attractive opportunities. Database marketing provides information about trends and changes in the market and that, in turn, enables you to plan your own product developments in line with those needs. Understanding the market's changing needs helps you to deal with issues such as:

- What direction should new product development take?

- What is the likely timetable for new product development?

- Have I got the skills and resources to meet future new product requirements?

- What are our customers' new product plans and how can we contribute to those?

- Can we help our customers develop new products that they would not otherwise be capable of?

UNDERSTANDING COMPETITORS

Do you know as much about your competitors as you would like to? Can you assess the likely impact of a competitor's advertising campaign? Is anyone responsible for assessing competitive activity?

Competitor assessment is easily overlooked and any information may simply be held by individuals. Competitive information can be valuable on planning future strategies and responding quickly to threats. The database can be used as a focal point for gathering information on competitive activity and making it available to key people. These are some of the issues you can review through the database:

- Key competitors by sector and individual customer.

- Competitors' market share and trends.

- Competitive pricing levels.

- Competitive promotional activity and expenditure.

- Details of customers lost to competitors.

- Details of gains from competitors.

- Attitudes to customers.

- Press coverage of competitors.

If direct sales operations are important to your company, database techniques can help to improve salesforce performance through the provision of comprehensive sales support information and stronger control.

The database can provide the salesforce with a wide range of information that builds a complete picture of customers and the way they respond to sales and marketing initiatives. The database can be used to provide the following information:

● Customer profile and contact information.

● Customer purchasing history.

● Any known problems.

● Individual sales or direct marketing initiatives and the response.

● Wider communications programmes or promotional activity within the customer's sector.

● Competitive activity on the account.

● Profitability of the account.

The database can also be used to improve salesforce control by providing reports and information on team and individual performance, sales costs and the effectiveness of sales support programmes. This information can be used as a basis for allocating sales resources, training, territory planning and developing other forms of support such as telesales. The database can be used to provide the following management information:

● The performance of different sales representatives.

● The overall performance of the sales team.

● The comparative performance of different sales channels such as field sales, telesales, distributors or agents.

● The impact of marketing campaigns on sales performance.

● Cost of sales.

● The effectiveness of different call patterns.

Database marketing helps you to prioritize sales activities and control sales costs by highlighting and quantifying profitable long-term market opportunities. The cost of winning new business can be high - involving research, prospecting, progress meetings, proposals and development costs as well as the administrative costs of opening new accounts and setting up procedures to handle the work. The information available through database marketing enables you to assess the likely success factors in target markets and make best use of your sales and marketing resources. You can also concentrate on maintaining relationships because there is a cost and a degree of risk in replacing a supplier. Customers are reluctant to change, or find there are considerable barriers to change, and this can help to reduce a company's sales and marketing costs. The emphasis is on providing a high quality, reliable service rather than developing new leads. Sales staff can concentrate on account development tasks and managing the teams of people who will provide support to the customer.

FAST TRACK

○ *Ensure that your sales team has full and easy access to the information they need.*

○ *Introduce a reporting mechanism that enables you to capture the management information you need from the salesforce.*

MANAGING MARKETING CAMPAIGNS

Many companies manage their marketing campaigns with simple measures such as the number of enquiries generated through an advertising campaign or the response rate to a direct mail-shot. While these measures continue to be valuable, they do not provide a broad picture of the impact of the campaign on the customer or the performance of other sales and marketing activities. By using database techniques, you can improve campaign evaluation as a basis for future planning. The database can be used to provide the following types of information:

● The number of leads and sales resulting from campaigns.

● The overall cost of sales by sector and individual customer.

● The contribution of a campaign.

● The cost of a response, lead or sale by different types of campaign.

● The effect of different messages or promotional offers on campaign effectiveness.

● Market penetration in relation to different levels of spend or different types of campaign.

- The effectiveness of different media.

- The relative performance of different elements within an integrated campaign.

In business-to-business and consumer marketing, regular contact and effective customer relationships are essential to long-term success. By using database marketing programmes to plan and monitor which customers to contact, when to contact them and what form the contact should take, you can build relationships that maintain the right level of control. This contact and control is important because it keeps the whole company close to the customer, helping to keep them up-to-date with the customers' changing business requirements. The regular contact available through database marketing also provides the opportunity to demonstrate customer care and take a proactive approach to customer relationships.

FAST TRACK

○ *Develop relevant measures for your sales and marketing activities.*

○ *Ensure that the information is available to marketing staff and marketing services agencies.*

improving long-term business performance

The long-term relationship with customers that is integral to the concept of database marketing is the basis for improving overall business performance.

- You can develop a long-term strategy that is based on a clear understanding of your customers' long-term needs.

- You can implement the strategy confident that you know who your customers will be in three to five years and confident that you can predict their levels of business.

- You can make product development and investment decisions confident that you have reduced the risk in the decision-making process.

- You can reduce costs by implementing continuous improvement processes that are based on an understanding of your customers' long-term needs.

- You should be able to increase levels of business without a corresponding rise in the cost of sales.

- You can reduce your skills development costs by investing in training that is geared to your customers' long-term needs.

is database marketing right for you?

The overall benefit of database marketing is that it reduces the risk in planning and implementing a long-term business strategy and enables you to take actions that will improve overall performance. If you are considering whether database marketing might benefit your business, consider these benefits.

DON'T FORGET!

Database marketing will help you:

- ○ *Improve frequency and quality of customer contact.*
- ○ *Build long-term customer retention.*
- ○ *Increase customer focus.*
- ○ *Understand and influence purchasing patterns.*
- ○ *Enjoy greater opportunities for repeat business.*
- ○ *Prioritize sales activities and control sales costs.*
- ○ *Focus your product planning.*
- ○ *Improve long-term business performance.*

2

data and marketing

This chapter looks at data and its contribution to the marketing process. It explains how data can be managed and how it can be used to improve sales and marketing performance. The costs of managing data and the range of database services are also examined.

the importance of data

Companies of varying sizes and at different stages of their development are using database marketing programmes to improve their business performance. Database marketing is now becoming a vital tool
for strategic marketing throughout the UK and Europe and is an essential part of a competitive marketing strategy.

Some statistics demonstrate the growing adoption of database and
related direct marketing techniques by marketing professionals.

Volume	284.5 million items – up 5% on 1993	
Expenditure	1993	£904 million
Proportion of marketing spend	1990/93	10/11%
	1984/89	7/9%

ATTITUDES TO DATABASE MARKETING

A survey of marketing managers and directors recorded the following
views:

- 9/10 marketers recognise database marketing as an important part
  of their marketing strategy.

- 42% currently use customer loyalty schemes; 55% said they would
  do so over the next 12 months.

- 71% handle database management in house.

In a recent survey of spending plans among business marketing executives, 65% of those surveyed said they planned to increase their
expenditure on direct marketing over the next three years. This is how
marketing directors plan to increase their budget allocation:

- Advertising   24%

- Direct marketing   65%

- Publications   23%

- Exhibitions   10%

- Public relations   17%

the benefits of using quality data

Quality data can offer your business a wide range of sales and marketing benefits, including:

- Higher response.
- Greater conversion.
- Ability to cross-sell.
- Opportunity to sell up.
- Increased customer loyalty.
- Greater customer retention.
- Improved customer service.
- Cost effectiveness.
- Targeted marketing.
- Measurable performance.
- Better segmentation.
- Identification of purchasing habits.
- Support for integrated marketing.

setting up a marketing database

At a fundamental level, many companies already hold a database in some form, but they may not be using it effectively to drive and support their marketing initiatives. This information might include:

- Purchase records.
- Enquiries and orders.
- Accounts details.
- Service records.

Often, this information is kept on separate databases or mechanical filing systems, but it provides important information to support sales and marketing initiatives and is too valuable to be simply stored. With the increasing importance now placed on database marketing, companies must understand how they can exploit their customer data in a planned way, rather than leave it locked up in a departmental filing system.

WATCH OUT!

Just because a company has a database, this does not mean that it is practising database marketing. This book will show how that data can be used to support the marketing process. However, before beginning any of the programmes, it is important to get the database right.

Data integrity is critical. Effective database marketing can only be achieved by ensuring the basics are in place and this means using accurate, appropriate and clean data. Using the latest database management software is useless if the database consists of outdated and unfocused lists of company names and addresses. Companies which fail to consider the accuracy of their data before embarking on a database marketing campaign could be wasting time, effort and money.

The implementation of a new database may require some fundamental changes to internal processes, such as the re-organisation of sales territories, new contact strategies or new sales techniques. That will require a fundamental change in a company's strategic thinking. It is therefore important to get the commitment of the senior management team as the original database marketing "champion" may move on to another task before the project is complete. Long-term management continuity is vital.

TRICKS OF THE TRADE

Although database marketing is a long-term investment in customer loyalty, the early stages of the project should be structured to demonstrate immediate benefits which, in turn, will maintain internal commitment and support.

The programme might begin with simple applications such as direct mail, but these could lead to more sophisticated developments such as relationship marketing programmes. You may consider talking to database experts either in your own company or from an outside consultancy. This will ensure that your programme is designed with long-term objectives in mind from the outset.

Database experts and consultants can also provide the "hand-holding" that may be necessary in the early stages. This advice and guidance covers a number of important activities:

● Cleaning, enhancing and profiling data.

● Understanding the available data to ensure that the market is fully exploited.

● Information on available hardware and software.

working with accurate data

HOW ACCURATE DATA INFLUENCES RESPONSE RATES Establishing your database is often the most difficult and certainly the most critical first step, but the way you use and maintain that data will determine the long-term benefits and the ultimate return on your investment. Without constant updating, any database will be a wasted asset.

The UK list manager, The Business Database, carried out research among 20 of the UK's top companies to identify the problems companies faced in working with business data. The key finding was that, apart from budget, accurate data is the most important factor in successful database marketing.

EXAMPLE

Interprint

Interprint Limited is one of the UK's most successful short-run colour printers and a confirmed user of direct marketing techniques. The company distributes around 150,000 mailing items every month to prospects and customers. The mailing programme includes A5 leaflets and full colour brochures, highlighting Interprint products, together with a newsletter that covers the latest developments and news of Interprint activities.

Over the last five years, Interprint has supplemented its in-house database of 60,000 customer names and addresses with over 70,000 business-to-business addresses each month. Interprint believes that the accuracy of its database has played a major part in achieving an above-average 2–2.5% response to its mailings.
○

HOW ACCURATE DATA QUANTIFIES MARKET POTENTIAL A company new to a market that wants to relocate or develop new sales territories can utilize different database marketing techniques to meet broader marketing objectives.

EXAMPLE

Kall Kwik Printing

Kall Kwik Printing, one of the UK's most successful franchise operations, used location-based data as a planning tool to improve the methods and validity of its research process for identifying suitable sites for franchisees. The data detailed the major concentrations of target businesses across the UK and cross-referenced it by business type. Kall Kwik was able to define the business community in target locations with a higher degree of accuracy and the process was more cost-effective. This type of profiling can be adapted to suit the majority of industry sectors and businesses of all sizes. ○

HOW ACCURATE DATA CAN MAXIMIZE MARKET POTENTIAL For start-up companies or companies moving to new locations where they have no established customer base, defining and reaching the new market is crucial to survival. Database marketing has proved consistently successful in building up customer databases from scratch, quickly and efficiently.

EXAMPLE

Annopak

A national wholesaler operating through a branch network, supported the launch of new branches with a direct marketing programme. The branches aimed to build a base of customers within a specific drive-time area and database techniques were used to reach that market. Annopak, a mailing house used data to analyze the area by the number of potential new business opportunities. By categorizing the data by post-code and SIC categories (see below), Annopak was able to pin-point sub-categories of potential prospects within the given area such as retailers, restaurants and public houses. The database yielded approximately 50,000 names and Annopak was then able to develop a series of tailored mailings which included brochures, promotional offers and personalised letters. ○

---

market segmentation options

There is a wide variety of data which can be tailored to the marketing needs of different types of companies. It includes:

- *Business name*
  This is the trading name of the company.

- *Business address*
  This includes the Royal Mail recognised post-town.

- *Post-code*
  Addresses can be fully post-coded against Royal Mail records. This is essential if they are to qualify for Mailsort discounts.

- *Telephone number*
  The business telephone number including the STD code can be used for segmentation.

- *Mailsort coding*
  Mailsort codes can be included on each data entry to enable the customer to reclaim appropriate discounts through Royal Mail.

- *Yellow Pages classifications*
  This categorizes businesses into around 2,700 different types.

- *Number of employees*
  This identifies companies by the number of employees based at each location.

- *SIC codes (1980 and 1992)*
  This classifies businesses into approximately 350 (SIC 1980) or 503 (SIC 1992) categories conforming to descriptions published by the Department of Trade and Industry and CSO.

- *New opportunities*
  A monthly file can be provided which identifies new business telephone subscribers. This enables companies to reach new start-up businesses in their first 12 months of operation.

- *Groups and sectors*
  This segmentation option groups Yellow Pages classifications together to target industries on a broader basis.

database development services

There are five main types of database development services that can be used to enhance a database.

DATA CLEANING

This service provides a vital health check on a company's data and can improve it to Royal Mail standards. A series of data assessment programmes are conducted to establish the accuracy of business data and full data cleaning is carried out with address enhancement in accordance with the Post Office's post-code files.

DATA ENHANCEMENT

This service enables companies to maximize the value of existing data by adding selective data to customer and prospect lists. This information includes:

- SIC 80 or SIC 92 codes.
- Yellow Pages classification.
- Yellow Pages business group and sector.
- Number of employees.
- Type of premises.
- Telephone number.
- Full address.

DATA PROFILING

Data profiling provides companies with breakdowns of businesses into a number of different categories, including:

- Type of business.
- Size of business.
- Geographic location.

DATA UPDATING

Research shows that the rate of change of business data is 48% per annum. An updating service can provide valuable information on changes such as:

- Business moves.

- New business start-ups.

- Changes in trading activities.

- Telephone, address or post-code changes.

the implications of data protection

WATCH OUT!

If you maintain personal information about one or more individuals on computer (personal information includes names and addresses) you must register your activities with The Data Protection Register. You must also comply with the requirements of the Data Protection Act

To comply you must:

- Show the nature of the data you hold.

- Describe the purpose for which the data is to be used, now and in the future.

If you fail to register, or use the data in ways that fall outside the scope of registration, you are committing a criminal offence and can be prosecuted. The main requirements of the Data Protection Act are summarized below.

- Information contained in personal data should be obtained and processed fairly and lawfully – there should be no attempt to mislead or deceive people providing information.

- Personal data should only be held for one or more specified lawful purposes – those purposes must be described on the Data Protection Register.

- The data should not be used or disclosed in any way that is incompatible with the purposes described in the Register.

- Personal data should be adequate, relevant and not excessive in relation to the registered purpose.

- Personal data should be accurate and kept up to date.

- Personal data should not be kept for longer than necessary for the registered purpose.

- Individuals are entitled to be informed whether data is held and are allowed access to that data. If appropriate, they can ask to have the data corrected or removed.

- The user should take appropriate security measures to protect the data.

planning your database marketing system

Quality data is the starting point for effective database marketing. To select the right system to manage your data, you need to be clear about how you will use it.

- How will it support your business obiectives?

- What benefits do you expect from the system?

- What are the main requirements for the system?

- What applications will you want to use it for?

- What improvements do you expect for each of the applications?

USING CONSULTANTS TO PLAN YOUR SYSTEM If you do not have the necessary skills in your own organization, you should consider using outside expertise to ensure that your database marketing programme is built on a firm base. A database consultant can help you to establish the requirements for your system and recommend the right hardware/software combination to match your needs.

FAST TRACK

Although you may have IT specialists within your organization, they may not be able to advise you on the business benefits of different systems.

Ideally, the consultant should have relevant experience in your market and should have a detailed understanding of the benefits of sales and marketing systems. In briefing a consultant, you should provide comprehensive information on your business and your sales and marketing operations, as well as the database requirements that were outlined earlier. Discussions with the consultant may help you to refine your requirements.

PREPARING A BUSINESS CASE FOR YOUR SYSTEM

A database marketing system represents a significant investment and it is important that it is fully evaluated. One of the important benefits of using database techniques is the improved understanding of customers and the opportunity to maximize lifetime customer value. The concept of lifetime customer value is described in detail in Chapter 4.

INTERNAL RESOURCES OR OUTSOURCING

While you may feel that an internal database gives you more control over your data, this may not be the cost-effective solution. Using an external supplier to maintain and manage your database can provide a number of important benefits:

- The database will not reduce the overall capacity of your internal systems.

- You will not have to recruit staff to manage the database.

- Your database will be managed by skilled specialists, possibly using more sophisticated systems.

- You can select a number of service options, including services to maintain your data.

DON'T FORGET!

Data has no value unless it is used to improve the performance of sales and marketing systems. As Chapter 1 showed, data can be used to support a wide range of sales and marketing opportunities. The rest of this book shows how the data can be applied.

3

integrated marketing campaigns

This chapter looks at the way different marketing activities relate to each other and shows how the database plays a central role in improving the performance of each activity and the overall campaign. In planning an integrated campaign, the database can be used to assess the communication needs of each sector and identify marketing or promotional activities that have, historically, proved effective. As the campaign runs, data from customer responses to specific sales or marketing actions can be used to fine tune messages or promotional offers. The chapter shows how to get full value from all the marketing tools you use and how to use the results from one campaign to improve the performance of others. To demonstrate the process, this chapter includes an example of the launch of a new insurance policy.

the scope of an integrated campaign

A wide-ranging marketing programme might include some or all of the following elements:

- Advertising.

- Direct mail.

- Telemarketing.

- Sales promotion and incentives.

- Salesforce communications.

- Local marketing support.

- Product information.

- Relationship marketing.

Traditional marketing strategies treat different marketing activities as separate unrelated entities, each of which might produce incremental results. The objectives and schedule for each of the elements is set separately and the programmes may be handled by separate departments which work with different agencies. This can lead to fragmentation and dilution of overall effectiveness such as:

- Different messages.

- Different creative treatment.

- Timing problems.

- Dilution of visual standards.

However, by using a database to record and monitor the results of each activity, you can identify the most successful elements and use them as a basis for future planning. What's more, the customer information on the database gathered through advertising or other activities can be used as a basis for direct marketing programmes. The relaunch of the Rover Metro shows how effective this approach can be.

EXAMPLE

Rover Metro relaunch

The Metro was launched in 1979, becoming the highest volume seller in Rover's history. The engineering of the car was fundamentally over-hauled in 1990, but external appearances were largely unchanged. In 1991, competitive pressure on the Metro increased with the launch of the Renault Clio and Peugeot 106. Sales share began to fall despite pricing activity. Integrated marketing agency KMM's (now known as Lintas i) first task when they were appointed by Rover in January 1992 was to halt and reverse this decline in share which had slipped to below 2%. The objective was immediately to lift share to more than 4% with a settled down rate in excess of 3%.

The strategy adopted by KMM was to highlight the changes that had been made to the car in a dramatic and intrusive way, in order to force a reappraisal of a car that most consumers thought they knew. To this end, extensive use was made of a road test conducted by Car Magazine.

An integrated campaign was developed consisting of 40-second television com-mercials, 48-sheet posters and a national press campaign featuring a direct res-ponse mechanism offering further information. Those who responded to this received their information pack containing a test drive incentive based on the offer of a range of Harrods' merchandise. This promotional offer was also carried through to point-of-sale.

Subsequently, the launch of two new Metro derivatives (a diesel engine and an automatic gearbox) was also handled via direct marketing and point-of-sale. The entire campaign was turned around in eight weeks from receipt of the brief to the TV commercial and first national press ad appearing.

The result of the campaign has been highly satisfactory. Metro's share of the industry volume rose from 1.9% to 4.3%, subsequently settling down to a share in excess of 3.5%. Previously Rover's highest ever response to a test drive incentive programme had been 7,000. The integrated campaign, despite the comparatively low profile of the Harrods' offer, generated over 13,500 test drive enquiries.

The total cost of the campaign was under £2.5 million and Rover estimated that the activity boosted profitability by over £7 million. Equally important, image track-ing studies show that in several key areas Metro's image has shifted favourably indi-cating a longer-term benefit from this essentially tactical programme. ○

As the example shows, without the support of the other marketing ele-ments, the advertising and direct mail programmes would have achieved results but together they reinforce each other to achieve real impact. In this case, the database was used to support and enhance a number of activities:

- Recording responses from advertising.

- Using the responses as a basis for a mailing campaign.

- Tracking the responses from the mailing campaign against subsequent sales.

- Measuring the cost per sale and assess the overall effectiveness of the campaign in financial terms.

- Tracking the changes in awareness and image resulting from the campaign.

developing an integrated campaign

The remainder of this chapter shows how different marketing activities contribute to the effectiveness of an integrated campaign and explains the role of the database at each stage.

The example is based on an insurance company that is introducing a "direct" service, ie offering customers products and services by telephone, to supplement the traditional route of agents or financial intermediaries. The proposition to the consumer is that the process of taking out a policy and making a claim is quicker, simpler and cheaper. Although the company sees potential in the direct route, it wants to compare results with traditional methods.

The database underpins the whole process by comparing results from different campaigns and building information on customers as a basis for cross-selling and planning other marketing activities to move the customer along a "campaign track" from prospect to loyal customer.

the overall strategy

The insurance company has a database of existing customers who have bought policies in the traditional way. The company uses its database to develop its overall strategy:

- It will generate a mailing list of existing customers to explain the changes.

- It will use advertising to provide new prospects who can be followed up by appropriate marketing.

- It will use prospect profiles to select the most suitable channels and marketing techniques.

- During the prospect conversion stage, it will use the database to assess the effectiveness of different marketing actions.

- When prospects have been converted, it will use the database to plan a long-term strategy for cross-selling other products and services.

- It will assess the performance of different channels.

advertising

The insurance company uses advertising in a number of different ways:

- As a national direct response medium to generate leads for a corporate direct marketing or telemarketing campaign.

- As a local direct response medium to generate leads for local follow-up by financial intermediaries.

- As part of a selective regional sales promotion campaign that offers prospects incentives for providing database information.

- As a local or regional joint campaign between the insurance company and selected financial intermediaries.

- As part of a national or regional consumer awareness campaign, with different weights of support to selected regions. This approach could also be used in test marketing.

- As part of a campaign to improve the level of local representation in selected regions. The insurance company could offer advertising as part of its local support package.

ADVERTISING AND THE DATABASE

The database can be used in the following ways:

- To assess which media were most effective in reaching the target audience.

- To assess how response levels compared in different media.

- To record customer data captured through the campaign.

The table below shows the type of publications that could be used in the campaign and the basic measures that could be used to assess the contribution of the media.

Type of publication	Enquiries	Sales	Cost per Enquiry
National and regional daily and Sunday newspapers with a personal finance section			
National and regional daily and Sunday newspapers with a motoring section			
Local daily or weekly newspapers, particularly those with a motoring or personal finance section			
National or local commercial radio stations			
Network or regional television			
Specialist personal finance publications			
Special interest car magazines			

direct mail

Direct mail is one of the most flexible tools in an integrated marketing programme. It can be used to reinforce the effectiveness of other marketing tools or it can be used alone in a variety of different ways. Direct mail advertising, for example, can be a viable alternative to press or broadcast media and it can be used to reach specific sectors of the market. In an integrated campaign, it can also be used to follow up prospects who request further information and it can be used to maintain effective contact and build long-term relationships with customers.

It could be used in the following ways:

- As a follow-up to the direct response advertising campaign. The advertisements provide information on warm prospects which can be used to form a database for future direct marketing programmes.

- To make differentiated offers to prospects who respond to the advertising campaign.

- To supplement the advertising campaign's coverage of different target markets. Direct mail can be used to reach sectors that cannot be reached efficiently by other media or to provide increased reach or frequency.

- To reinforce the impact of the advertising campaign by selective follow-up.

DIRECT MARKETING AND THE DATABASE

At this stage, the database can be used in the following ways:

- To track the responses in different sectors.

- To refine information on existing customers and prospects generated through advertising enquiries.

- To assess the effectiveness of different campaign themes and approaches.

- To assess how response levels compared in different campaigns.

- To record customer data captured through the campaign.

- To provide information for planning telemarketing or sales follow-up.

- To compare the costs of reaching prospects through different channels.

USING THE DATABASE TO SEGMENT THE DIRECT MARKETING CAMPAIGN

By analyzing the customer and prospect lists on the database, the insurance company is able to target its mailing campaign more precisely. These were some of the mailings it ran:

● New product information sent to existing policyholders.

● New product information sent to lapsed policyholders.

● Targeted information sent to specific types of existing policyholder.

● Information sent to a database of prospects generated through consumer advertising.

● Information sent to a database of prospects compiled by local financial intermediaries.

● Information sent to a database of prospects generated by other methods.

USING THE DATABASE TO VARY THE OFFER

Direct mail allows you to approach new prospects in a variety of different ways, using different creative approaches or varying the promotional offer. The insurance company planned a diverse direct mail campaign which included the following elements:

● A series of special offers targeted at the age and lifestyle of the recipient:
  – Young drivers were offered discounts on car audio systems and information on autosport
  – Family motorists were offered discounts on car security systems or membership of a motoring organization.

● Holiday breaks were offered to customers who replied within a certain timescale.

● Follow-up mailings to customers who had not responded within a certain timescale.

● Welcome mailings to prospects who responded or opened a policy.

● A special launch pack with varied incentives aimed at financial intermediaries.

In each case, the information on prospects, their response and the success of the offer were available from the database for planning, analysis and further follow-up.

telemarketing

The insurance company uses telemarketing to supplement the advertising and direct mail campaigns. It can be used to handle a number of different tasks:

- Providing a point of response for queries generated through advertising or direct marketing campaigns.

- Obtaining information from respondents as a basis for future database marketing.

- Building direct sales to prospects over the telephone.

- Acquiring new financial intermediaries or keeping current advisers up-to-date with new products.

- Maintaining contact with current customers and using the relationship to launch new products.

- Generating leads from unqualified mailing lists and following up direct marketing programmes.

- Winning back lapsed customers by introducing them to new products which may be of greater interest.

- Following up leads generated through advertising or direct marketing or via financial intermediaries.

- Carrying out market research using the surveys to establish consumer response to the products or to sales incentives.

- Maintaining contact with both consumers and financial intermediaries as part of a relationship marketing programme.

TELEMARKETING AND THE DATABASE

All of those functions depend on effective database information:

- To provide telesales staff with customer information so that they can handle customer calls more effectively and productively.

- To track the responses in different sectors.

- To further refine the customer and prospect information.

- To compare the results of direct marketing programmes with and without telemarketing support.

sales promotion and incentives

Many companies are now realizing that sales promotion and incentives must be integrated with other above and below-the-line activities. By tracking responses to different promotions and capturing customer data and purchasing patterns, the database can be used to add value to sales promotion programmes. In the example, the insurance company uses promotions and incentives to reinforce other campaign elements.

SALES PROMOTION AND THE DATABASE

The database can be used in the following ways:

- To track the responses to different promotions.

- To capture data from promotions.

- To assess the impact of different types of incentives.

- To refine the targeting of other promotional offers.

TACTICAL CONSUMER PROMOTION

Sales promotion can be integrated with advertising and direct marketing campaigns to raise response rates for both initial enquiries and conversions. For example, including a group of special offers which encourage initial enquiry, signing an agreement and paying the first premium. The database can be used to track the effectiveness of different types of promotion and to show how they contribute to the success of the overall campaign. The promotions can be used in the following ways:

- To support lead generation programmes for direct marketing and telemarketing.

- To encourage prospects to provide database information.

- In a test marketing programme to assess the effectiveness of different media and promotional combinations.

- To target different groups of consumers with special offers that reflect different lifestyles. The section on direct marketing gave examples of targeted offers for young drivers and family motorists that formed an integral part of the direct marketing programme.

STRATEGIC SALES PROMOTION

Strategic sales promotion can be integrated with relationship marketing programmes to support branding opportunities and build customer loyalty. For example, special offers can be developed to encourage existing policy holders to trade up to higher value policies or to try other products in the group. In each case, the database provides the information that allows the offers to be highly targeted. A strategic campaign can operate in a number of ways by·

- Offering customers and prospects special services or other offers that support core brand qualities.

- Rewarding existing customers for renewal and repeat business.

- Using strategic promotions to reactivate lapsed accounts.

- Offering customers high quality incentives to support the marketing of higher value products.

- Structuring programmes to suit different customer spending levels.

INCENTIVE PROGRAMMES

Incentive programmes can be used to focus the salesforce and financial advisers on important marketing activities. Sales incentives should be directly related to the current campaigns and can be both tactical and strategic. The database is used to identify the areas where incentives are required to improve penetration and should also be used to measure the effectiveness of the incentive.

The insurance company used a number of tactical incentives, including:

- Product sales incentives based on new business generation and policy sales, with a structured scheme related to the number of conversions. This would ensure that the salesforce made the best use of the leads generated through direct marketing and advertising and concentrated on building higher levels of new sales.

- Structured incentives for target market sales. If the company wants to increase penetration in specific sectors, tie the incentive programme to sales in niche markets and integrate direct marketing and telemarketing activity to increase the chances of success.

- Short-term incentives to achieve revenue targets.

- Incentives linked to generation of database information, even though the prospect may not purchase immediately.

salesforce communications

Database information can be used to improve salesforce performance. Ongoing salesforce communications are essential to ensure that they are always up-to-date with developments and committed to making the most of the marketing opportunities available. The salesforce can be the most important point of contact with the customer and it is vital that they are fully aware of all the support that is available to them.

THE SALESFORCE AND THE DATABASE

The database can be used in the following ways to:

- Ensure that the salesforce has access to comprehensive customer information.

- Compare sales performance with different levels of marketing support.

- Provide high quality sales leads.

- Track sales history resulting from leads.

DIFFERENT TYPES OF SALESFORCE COMMUNICATIONS

Salesforce communications can take a number of forms:

- Information on the advertising and direct marketing programmes that are currently operating.

- Leads that are generated from advertising and direct marketing campaigns.

- Information on the consumer sales promotion and incentive programmes that are operating with full operational details so that they can explain them to customers and deal with any queries.

- Clear guidelines on the information that is needed to set up the customer database marketing operation. This ensures that the database can be used to complement future salesforce activity and the salesforce should be told how they will benefit from the information they are providing.

- Information on all the database marketing operations that are being carried out with their own customer base. This keeps the salesforce up-to-date with all the contact that is going on between them and ensures that there is no misunderstanding or duplication.

local marketing support

The insurance company had a network of financial advisers, with their own local client base and it is essential that the local advisers have the information and the support to deliver a high standard of customer service. This support can take a number of forms:

- Using direct marketing and local advertising to generate leads for local outlets.

- Providing customer information to local outlets so that they can build relationships with local customers.

- Co-operative programmes with local independent advisers to ensure an integrated approach in the local market.

THE DATABASE AND LOCAL SUPPORT

The database can be used in the following ways to:

- Assess the impact of different levels of marketing support on different local markets.

- Compare the performance of different local advisers.

- Provide customer data by individual adviser to support local direct marketing.

product information

Product information is important to insurance customers and it must be integrated with other communications elements. The database helps to track whether customers are getting the right information and how they responded. As part of the customer communications process, product information is used extensively:

- In response to requests generated via advertisements, direct marketing or enquiries from local advisers or local outlets.

- As part of a relationship marketing programme to keep customers up-to-date with commercial or product developments.

- As support material for the salesforce, local outlets or local advisers so that they can provide their customers with information.

THE DATABASE AND PRODUCT INFORMATION
The database is used in the following ways to:

- Identify information needs.

- Monitor response to product information.

relationship marketing

Relationship marketing is a fundamental activity that supports all other marketing activities. Relationship marketing has customer retention as its main objective. It recognizes that it is more profitable to retain and grow business with existing customers than to keep on winning new clients.

RELATIONSHIP MARKETING AND THE DATABASE
The database can be used in the following ways to:

- Provide information on customers' purchasing patterns and response to marketing actions.

- Develop a future strategy for product and service offers.

- Help select the media and marketing actions that are most effective.

- Help maintain the right level of contact.

- Measure the effectiveness of campaigns.

CUSTOMERS FOR LIFE Retaining customers for life is the ultimate aim of relationship marketing programmes and it is a concept that is particularly important in the financial services sector. Insurance companies recognize that their customer needs change through their lives and therefore it is important to retain constant contact. This means two major changes for the insurance company:

- Changing the role of the salesforce from new business getters to consultants who advise their customers on long-term planning.

- Building and utilizing a database to ensure that a targeted approach can be made to each customer.

Relationship marketing is based on regular, quality customer contact with information that reflects customers' needs. To ensure that the database fully supports relationship marketing, it is essential that the following actions are taken.

WATCH OUT!

○ *Lead generation programmes utilizing advertisements and direct marketing are designed to provide information for the database.*

○ *Follow-up direct marketing and telemarketing utilizes information from the initial enquiry to provide the customer with targeted communications and offers.*

○ *Promotional and incentive activities are targeted to customers' needs, and the current stage of account development. Incentives can be used to encourage commitment to first purchase, trade-up to a higher value policy or to cross-sell other products in the range.*

○ *Planned direct marketing and telemarketing can be utilized at regular intervals to ensure regular contact with customers to keep them informed or to arrange appointments with consultants.*

increasing marketing flexibility

Throughout this chapter, we have referred to testing and assessment of marketing activities. The following section looks at this in more detail.

Database marketing techniques allow you to carry out tests on the effectiveness of your integrated marketing programmes by comparing the results of different strategies or techniques. In direct mail, for example, campaigns can incorporate different messages or offers, different prices and a range of other variables. It can also show you how to mix and match different campaign elements.

This has two important benefits. It allows you to assess the effectiveness of different approaches and also allows you to fine tune the campaign to suit the needs of different markets.

TESTING THE CAMPAIGN

What sort of tests should you carry out before the main campaign?

Part of the flexibility of direct marketing is that you can test your approach before committing resources to the full campaign. There are a number of variables that can be tested:

● The offer.

● The creative approach.

● The target audience.

● The response mechanism.

● Frequency and timing.

● Integration with other communications programmes.

The test campaign can be carried out in a number of ways:

● On a representative sample of the target market.

● In a defined sales or geographical territory.

● To a particular sector of the target market.

The most effective test campaign is the one that achieves the highest response levels.

PLANNING SPLIT CAMPAIGNS

Should you run a single campaign or utilize a split approach?

Testing your campaign may reveal that different approaches work more effectively in different market sectors. This is an example of a split campaign.

A company sponsored a seminar for senior executives at which recognized consultants reviewed new developments in the market. To ensure effective coverage of a diverse market, the seminar invitations mailed by the company included sector-specific letters which included the most important benefits of the seminar for each sector. The campaign was supported by press releases in specialist magazines covering market sectors where the company was not well known. The campaign also featured two different response mechanisms – a priority pre-paid reply card mailed to prospects where the company was seeking further contact information, and a second version featuring a FreePhone number for registration aimed at prospects and customers already on the company's database.

TARGET RESPONSE LEVELS

What results do you want from your campaign?

In the long term, a campaign may increase awareness, improve customer relations or cut the cost of sales. However, the simplest and most immediate measure of a direct marketing campaign is the response level it achieves. In setting your target response levels, you should aim for a realistic figure that is within your budget:

- Response levels as low as 1 or 2% are regarded as the industry norm.

- Response rates in the region of 5% are regarded as high.

- Response rates in the 10–20% region have been reported by companies who have integrated other forms of marketing communications.

There are a number of factors that can affect the level of response, including:

- Price.

- Quality of the mailing list.

- The promotional offer.

- Quality of copy and design.

Remember that the larger your target market, the more your overall costs will increase in relation to response levels. The costs are not just based on the costs of the initial mailing, you also have to consider:

- The cost of handling the response – FreePhone costs and telephone resources, costs of FreePost services.

- The cost of meeting the response – supplying and distributing the material that is requested.

- The cost of servicing the response – sales or telemarketing costs in dealing with the potential volume of new business.

DON'T FORGET!

An integrated strategy can help you get better value from your sales and marketing activities. The use of database techniques will:

○ *Ensure that you make best use of the customer information that is generated by different campaign activities.*

○ *Help you to assess the effectiveness of different campaign elements.*

○ *Allow campaigns to be tailored to the needs of individual sectors.*

○ *Help you to focus sales and marketing resources on the most important sectors.*

4

relationship marketing

This chapter looks at the way in which database techniques can be used to support different types of relationship marketing programmes. Relationship marketing programmes are not just a form of sales incentive, they demonstrate that your organisation cares about its customers and is prepared to reward loyalty.

the scope of relationship marketing

Increasing customer retention is a key business objective, because customers who are satisfied with the level and quality of service they receive are likely to continue buying from the same company. This degree of loyalty can be reinforced by relationship marketing programmes which reward customers for their loyalty in a way that further enhances customer service. Relationship marketing programmes can take many different forms from simple concepts like discounts on repeat purchases, incentives for multiple purchases to more complex frequent user programmes which provide multi- level rewards for customers who continue to use a service.

Behind effective relationship marketing programmes is a database that builds up an increasingly detailed picture of individual customers and their purchasing habits. The information allows you to target specific groups of customers with relevant offers and increase their value over the long term

**TRICKS OF
THE TRADE**

According to the Scandinavian airline, SAS, success in business depends not on selling the first airline ticket, car or financial product to the customer, but selling the fourth or fifth product to the same customer because they felt you had treated them well. Part of the process is knowing what that customer wants. Technology allows you to build up information on customers and use it to treat them as individuals. Every customer has lifetime value. A young inexperienced business traveller who would not normally receive special treatment has the potential to offer another 35 years' worth of business. It is therefore important to record and use that customer's buying patterns and preferences from the outset and keep making them offers that reward and build their loyalty.

the importance of relationship marketing programmes

Relationship marketing programmes are important in the following scenarios:

- Customers use the service frequently and the market is competitive.

- The programme proves to be an important differentiator.

- The programme provides an incentive to high levels of repeat purchase. Customers may use the product or service more frequently to gain additional points or prizes in the incentive programme.

- The incentive or reward itself provides an opportunity to demonstrate high levels of customer service. A frequent hotel user programme, for example, gives the customer an assured reservation, fast reception and a range of information to help make the traveller's life easier.

- The company is competing with other suppliers who offer similar services but do not have a customer service policy.

- The programme forms an integral part of the product or service offering.

EXAMPLE

Brooke Bond club collection

Club members are recruited off the pack through telephone hotlines or by door-to-door packs which include money-off coupons, free gift promotions and special starter tokens to get the collection underway. Members receive a welcome pack that includes a catalogue and personalized incentives. Through the Club, the company can build information on customer preferences and purchasing patterns for future direct marketing. ○

EXAMPLE

Frequent flyer

Frequent flyer programmes run by the major airlines are good examples of a long-term customer loyalty programme. The programmes are focused primarily on business travellers who travel regularly throughout the year. Although they are not spending their own money on travel, they are likely to select an airline that offers them the right level of service and convenience with an additional bonus if the airline includes a personal reward for loyalty.

North West Airlines, for example, uses customer information to make tailored offers and fill empty flights. As an example, it identified flyers who took ski trips and had high points totals. They were offered a special ski trip for a low price plus 10,000 collector points. This not only helped to build customer loyalty, it also filled the aeroplane.

British Airways Executive Club offers structured rewards to different groups of customers, according to their overall use of airline services. The scheme includes access to preferential seating, arrangements with hotels and car hire companies, and access to executive airport lounges. ○

In this type of programme, the database can be used to analyze purchasing patterns, identify frequent users and assess the impact of different offers on their purchasing patterns and loyalty. For example, to support the frequent buyer programmes, this is the type of information that should be collected:

● Customer information.

● Type of purchase.

● Date and value of purchase.

● Relevant marketing activities.

● Location.

● Frequency of purchase.

● Impact of special offers.

PROGRAMME OBJECTIVES

A customer retention programme would have the following business objectives:

- Reflect the high standard of customer service available.

- Offer customers a valuable reward or incentive for the continued relationship.

- Improve customer convenience as well as providing a reward.

- Motivate customers to remain loyal to the company.

- Provide high levels of customer information as a basis for database marketing programmes and future product development.

The more information you have on customers and their preferences, the more precisely you can meet these objectives.

WATCH OUT!

Don't forget to keep your information up-to-date. Nothing annoys customers more than the wrong details or offers that are irrelevant to them.

FREQUENT BUYER PROGRAMMES

Frequent buyer programmes that also accumulate information on customers are a powerful combination that strengthen the impact of customer focus programmes.

Frequent buyer programmes can be used to build a more complete picture of customers as a basis for detailed customer focus. A smart card can provide detailed knowledge on purchasing patterns that provides a basis for cross-selling other products and services or tailoring products and services to the customer.

EXAMPLE

Building retail loyalty

Retailer Argos operates a programme called **Premier Points** which issues points to customers for every ten pence they spend. The points are accumulated via a smart card and the customer can use the points to pay for other purchases. Smart card technology is also increasingly used by petrol retailers as a tie in to their collector schemes. Instead of collecting vouchers or tokens, points are accumulated via the card. Multiple food retailers like Tesco are also beginning to use a similar scheme to reward high spending customers. ○

using relationship programmes to cross-sell

How can you make the make the most of long-term customers? In financial services the core product is often a current account, but that provides the opportunity to market a range of products and services that change through a customer's lifetime, as this example shows.

EXAMPLE

Lifetime potential of a financial services customer

○ Current account   ○ Savings account

○ Personal loans   ○ Mortgage

○ Life assurance   ○ Pension

Behind this programme is a database that provides a complete picture of the customer:

● Age.

● Personal details.

● Credit reference details.

● Marital status.

● Children.

● Income.

● Household details.

● Other products or services bought from the institution.

● Response to product or service offers.

WATCH OUT!

Many financial services organisations have failed to take advantage of that type of opportunity because they have maintained customer information on different types of database that were driven by operational requirements.

customer clubs

If you want to make your customers feel welcome, make them members of a club and offer them benefits that reward their loyalty. A club is one of the most effective forms of relationship marketing, helping you to strengthen relationships with your customers and focusing activities on them.

Like the smart card information and data from other frequent buyer programmes, club information can be used as the basis for planning future targeted marketing activities. Single clubs can become a series of specialist clubs to meet specific requirements identified through the database.

● Ensure that you capture basic customer data on membership application forms.

● Track members' purchasing patterns and use this to make targeted offers.

● Consider using smart cards to improve data capture.

● Monitor the response to club offers.

● Segment your club database where possible to improve targeting even further.

SETTING OBJECTIVES

The key business objectives for a customer club are to:

● Secure customer loyalty in a competitive market.

● Build partnership with customers.

● Raise awareness of the company.

● Increase levels of quality contact with customers.

● Improve understanding of customer needs.

There are a number of scenarios when clubs are important.

Scenario	Example
When your customers make regular high value purchases and you want to retain their business	British Airways Executive Club and other frequent traveller clubs
When you have customers in a specific age group and you wish to retain their loyalty for life	Young savers clubs
When members pay a single annual fee for a service and you wish to retain their membership	Motoring organisations such as the AA and RAC
When there is an opportunity to make regular offers and sel relatedl products to specific groups of consumers with special interests	Book clubs or wine clubs
When there is an opportunity to differentiate a product or service by offering customers added value services that enhance the basic product or service	User groups
When there is an opportunity to offer regular subscribers special benefits	Sunday Times readers' discount card

The format of a customer club is extremely flexible and it is suitable for consumer, business-to-business and service markets.

PUTTING A CLUB INTO OPERATION

The process is illustrated by an example of a club run by a vehicle refinishing manufacturer, known as Colour Club. The club was launched by a combination of direct marketing and salesforce activity. Customers were offered membership of the club plus a range of benefits in return for an annual subscription.

The customer database was used to identify prospects for the club and the database was, in turn, enhanced by the information provided by members. Members were asked to provide information on:

● The size of their business.

● The number of technical staff.

● The average number of vehicles they repaired.

● Their use of refinishing paint.

This information was used to develop specific club offers and to provide a targeted product information service that reflected individuals' needs.

EXAMPLE

The Colour Club

The benefits included:

○ An updated edition of a colour yearbook - an easy to use reference guide to refinishing colours. This single guide would replace a cumbersome system of multiple reference books that had to be updated by the bodyshop.

○ Exclusive access to a colour hotline which provided members with technical information or advice and guidance whenever they needed it.

○ Training vouchers - members received discounts off colour skills courses.

○ Regular technical bulletins that offered useful advice.

As well as the technical support provided through the club, members were also offered privileged discounts on the company's products together with a range of social activities that increased personal contact and added further value to the club. ○

customers for life

By understanding your customers' lifetime value, you can be selective about who you try to keep, as well as who you try to attract.

- A 5% increase in customer retention could create a 125% increase in profits.

- A 10% increase in retailer retention can translate to a 20% increase in sales.

- Extending customer lifecycles by three years could treble profits per customer.

WHAT IS CUSTOMER LIFETIME VALUE? Customer lifetime value is how much your customers are worth to you over the length of time that they are your customers. For example, the bank customer who has a high monthly salary paid into his account each month, but immediately transfers spare funds into his building society account and takes out a car loan with another organization is not worth a lot to his bank. The lifetime for customers will vary from industry to industry and from brand to brand within a single organization.

You can assume that the lifetime of customers has come to an end when their contribution becomes so small as to be insignificant, unless of course you take steps to revitalize them.

- A good customer is a long-term customer who regularly buys a profitable product and who has bought recently.

- A new customer may be the best customer of all since their lifetime value has yet to be realized.

- An old customer who does not buy regularly, and has not bought recently, is probably not a customer at all.

- A lapsed customer who has been re-recruited often behaves like a new customer.

HOW TO CALCULATE LIFETIME VALUE In a consumer business, customer lifetime value is calculated, in practice, by analyzing the behaviour of a group of customers who have the same recruitment date. The group could consist of:

- Specific types of customers, for example in the same socio-economic group.

- Customers recruited from the same source.

- Customers who bought the same types of products.

In a business-to-business environment, a similar approach can be used. You could:

- Isolate particular customers and examine them individually.

- Analyze the behaviour of different groups, segmenting your customer database by factors such as industry, annual turnover or staff numbers.

Calculating lifetime value should be straightforward. The basic calculation has three stages.

1 Identify your discrete group of customers for tracking.

2 Record (or estimate) each revenue and cost for this group of customers by campaign or season.

3 Calculate the contribution by campaign or season.

EVALUATING A CAMPAIGN

Take a group of customers who were recruited through a direct response press advertising campaign in spring 1990 and track their expenditure to date.

Campaign	Total customer expenditure	Total marketing costs	Total contribution
Spring 1990	£50,000	£45,000	£5,000
Total '90	£75,000	£60,000	£15,000
Total '91	£85,000	£65,000	£20,000
Total '92	£92,000	£68,500	£23,500
Total '93	£107,000	£81,000	£26,000
Total '94	£115,000	£86,000	£29,000
Overall total	£524,000	£405,500	£118,500

You then divide the total contribution by the number of customers in the group. Say there are 1000 customers, then the average lifetime value per customer is £1,185 to date.

This is a simplistic approach to start you thinking about each customer's value. Other factors can be introduced to make the calculation more relevant to your business.

In a business-to-business environment, you may feel that it is your sales representatives who generate sales. In this case, you should include:

- The representative's "running costs".

- The cost of any centrally-produced sales support material.

Your company may offer different products or brands which are marketed under different cost centres. If a customer belongs to more than one cost/profit centre, you have a choice of approaches:

- Examine customers of each brand and ignore multi-purchases.

- Build a more detailed model that combines and allocates the cumulative costs as well as the cumulative profit in the appropriate proportions.

**USING CUSTOMER
LIFETIME VALUES**
Customer lifetime values can be used as the basis for four important calculations:

1 Setting target customer acquisition costs.

2 Allocating acquisition funds.

3 Selecting acquisition offers.

4 Supporting customer retention activities.

**Setting target
customer
acquisition costs**
If you believe that a customer is worth more than one sale, the allowable cost can be greater than the cost allowed for the first sale - the classic loss-leader approach to customer acquisition. However, overspending on customer acquisition can also be ruinous. A reasonable calculation is to recruit only from those sources that yield new customers at less than half the estimated lifetime value.

On that basis, the worst sources will have a cost per customer close to a lifetime value, while the average cost per customer should be far lower.

Allocating acquisition funds

Different recruitment sources will provide customers with different lifetime values. Once you have identified those values, you can then choose to spend more on the best sources. Lifetime value can also be applied when allocating funds between customer acquisition and customer reactivation.

Selecting acquisition offers

The lifetime value of a customer may depend on the type and value of their initial purchase. In turn, this can lead to decisions about which products and offers to use when advertising externally or when considering how to upgrade existing customers.

Supporting customer retention activities

Once you know what the typical lifetime value of your groups of customers is, you can decide how hard to work at retaining them. It is not a foregone conclusion that all customers are worth having. You should therefore tailor your "back-end" activities to those who are most valuable to you.

Relationship marketing programmes need not involve a major investment. The main investment is in selling the concept to customers. Programmes require careful administration to ensure that customers receive the highest standards of service, therefore training in programme administration skills will be important. It is essential that adequate resources are committed to the programme because quality customer relationships are essential to the success of a company's marketing.

- *Identify the business benefits.*
- *Assess the costs of each relevant programme.*
- *Appoint a programme co-ordinator.*
- *Research customer requirements.*
- *Refine the contents of each programme.*
- *Develop effective launch strategies.*
- *Ensure high levels of customer awareness.*
- *Ensure that customers continue to receive high levels of benefit.*

5

building partnerships

This chapter explains how the database can help you to identify partnership opportunities and improve the way you manage relationships with key accounts. The process of building partnerships can overcome competitive threats and increase the level of business from key accounts.

The book has shown how the increased customer focus of database marketing strengthens relationships with customers and helps to maintain account control in a competitive marketplace. The logical conclusion to this process is partnership – a way of doing business in which supplier and customer trade with each other to achieve mutual business objectives. Partnership replaces the traditional buyer/supplier relationship with a degree of co-operation and trust and utilizes each partner's skills to improve overall competitiveness.

Information, understanding and effective communications are key to the success of partnership, and therefore database marketing techniques play a key role in building and maintaining partnership. Effective database techniques allow you to track communications with key decision-makers and influencers within partner organisations and also identify opportunities to cross-sell other products and services.

partnership in action

BUILDING RELATIIONSHIPS An energy supplier and a high-volume electricity user co-operate on process developments that enable the customer to reduce overall manufacturing costs and provide the energy supplier with a long-term supply contract that is not dependent on price negotiations.

CO-OPERATING TO WIN BUSINESS A graphic design consultancy and an architectural practice co-operate to win a major retail refurbishing contract. Both partners utilize each other's specialist skills to develop a package of services that provides the ultimate customer with the most effective solution.

ADDING VALUE A car transportation company develops a three-way partnership with car manufacturers and car dealers. As well as providing the basic function of vehicle delivery from plant to dealership, the transport company provides services such as management information to improve communications between manufacturer and dealer, and professional vehicle preparation which helps both manufacturer and dealer improve customer satisfaction. The transport company develops a long-term relationship with the manufacturer, and both manufacturer and dealer improve their competitiveness.

IMPROVING LOCAL MARKETING PERFORMANCE A vehicle paint supplier develops a partnership programme to provide local distributors with skills and systems to improve their business management, marketing and customer service performance. By installing computers and business management systems in its branches, the manufacturer helps to build brand loyalty and improve the quality of service given to the ultimate customer – the bodyshop. The distributor has an opportunity to improve the performance of his own local business.

DEVELOPING A JOINT MARKET A petrochemical company co-operates with manufacturing customers to develop the market for a new plastic piping system. By providing high levels of technical and manufacturing support, the petrochemical company ensures that manufacturers understand how to make the best use of the new material. By developing joint product marketing initiatives, the partners are able to educate large-scale users in local government and the utilities of the cost and operational benefits of the new product. As a result, the petrochemical manufacturer increases the market for its new material and builds stronger relationships with customers, while the manufacturers expand the market for their products.

SPREADING THE RISK

A computer company and a management consultancy work in partnership to win a major health authority computer contract. Both parties realize that a successful computerization programme depends, not just on the best computer solution, but on careful assessment of long-term objectives and the establishment of the right management structure to utilize and manage the computer system. Without a supporting infrastructure, the computer system might have become a "white elephant". Close co-operation between both partners ensures that the ultimate customer – the health authority – obtains the right solution and that the partners develop a reputation that enhances their professional credibility.

REDUCING COSTS

An industrial component manufacturer and an engineering company co-operate on a joint development programme to reduce "through-life" costs of a number of key components. The component manufacturer contributes technical expertise and a close understanding of the engineering company's own customers, while the engineering company provides the component supplier with advice on improving the quality and cost-effectiveness of its manufacturing processes. The component supplier ensures long-term customer loyalty, while the energy company reduces its overall costs.

BUILDING LINKS THROUGH TECHNOLOGY

A travel company introduces a computerized enquiry and reservation system for independent travel agents. The system replaces slow manual systems of obtaining information and booking tickets, and enables independent travel agents to compete effectively with larger multiple travel groups who have access to a corporate reservation system. The travel agents are in a stronger position to win business, while the travel company builds the loyalty of the independent travel agent and improves the quality of service to the consumer.

DIFFERENTIATING A SERVICE A car insurance company wishes to improve its service to policy holders by offering quality services on body repairs and windscreen replacement. The insurance company works in partnership with leading companies in each sector, helping them to set up business processes and customer reception facilities that will ensure the highest standards of customer service. The specialist suppliers get access to larger markets and higher levels of business, while the insurance company is able to improve its cost position by offering policy holders added value and differentiating its services from price competitors.

why partnership is important

This brief outline of partnership cases shows that partnership is relevant to many different types of business – small and large manufacturers, sub-contractors, consultancies, distributors and retail outlets. In none of these cases were there formal contractual arrangements, although suppliers had to satisfy tight performance standards. Partnership evolved or occurred because both partners recognized the business benefits that would result. The relationships were based on a detailed understanding of each other's business and highly targeted communications. These are the key database tasks in considering partnership opportunities.

FAST TRACK

○ *Analyze sales and customer information.*

○ *Assess the value of sales to key customers.*

○ *Assess your customers' supply position.*

○ *Research customer requirements.*

○ *Assess competitive threats.*

○ *Analyze customer attitudes to your business.*

○ *Analyze customer markets.*

○ *Understand customer strategies.*

○ *Assess your value to your customers' business.*

database marketing

SALES AND CUSTOMER INFORMATION

Information is readily available in your own customer records that can help you to assess the opportunities for partnership. Does your database allow you to answer the following questions·

● What are their major markets?

● What are their most important products?

● What new products have they introduced in the last year?

● What are their plans for growth?

● What problems have they identified in their marketplace?

● What are the success factors in their market?

● Who are their main competitors?

Customer analysis doesn't just depend on database information. You can get similar information from other sources:

● Ask your salesforce to provide a profile of your most important customers, using the questions in the section above.

● Maintain a file of press cuttings on your customers' activities using their trade publications as a source.

● Build a file of corporate and product literature on your customers' competitors and look for press information on their market.

This information helps to build a profile of the direction your customer's business is taking and it should prompt you to ask "How could we help this customer overcome problems, realize opportunities or meet objectives? How could that strengthen our position and make us an important supplier?"

VALUE OF SALES TO KEY ACCOUNTS

Marketing textbooks suggest that there is a recurring pattern in the customer profiles of small and large organizations. It is based on Pareto analysis and suggests that around 80% of turnover comes from 20% of customers. In other words, all businesses have a small number of large customers whose purchases shape their own prospects. Although size alone is not a criterion for partnership status, it is essential to protect your customer base by building stronger relationships with those key customers. The first stage is to analyze your customer records in the database:

● Who are your largest customers?

- What percentage of your business do they represent?

- How dependent are you on their business continuing at the same level or growing?

- Which of the large customers has the strongest growth prospects?

- Is there a risk that any of the customers might defect to competitors?

- How long have they been doing business with you?

- How strong is the relationship with key decision-makers?

- How have levels of business changed over the past three years?

- Are there any significant developments which have affected these changes?

- What percentage of those customers' business do you handle?

- How could you increase your share?

WATCH OUT!

Larger customers are likely to be already receiving higher levels of service to maintain or grow the business, but partnership status will require a different set of relationships and you need to be certain that you have the resources to support and develop these accounts without putting your other major accounts at risk or upsetting the overall balance of your business.

YOUR CUSTOMERS' SUPPLY POSITION

The database may give you the specific information on purchasing history, but you also need to qualify this with qualitative information to plan your strategy.

Use the information in your customer records and ask your salesforce to assess your supply position:

- What percentage of the product do you supply?

- How does that compare with your competitors' share?

- How important is your product to the customer's business?

- Does your product have any specific features or benefits that cannot be substituted easily?

If a customer is dependent on you for supplies that are essential to its competitive ability, that may put you in a strong position to influence the direction of the relationship.

● Is your customer's demand for the product likely to grow?

● Could you meet the increased demand from your own resources or would your customer need to use other sources?

● Can you reduce your costs so that your product is more competitive?

● Can you add value to the product so that the customer obtains better value for money?

This analysis will indicate how closer relationships could benefit your business and your customer's. It will help you decide how to pitch your business proposals and how to align your business to your customer's needs.

RESEARCHING CUSTOMER REQUIREMENTS

Supply vulnerability may not be the only factor in your favour. Your customers may want access to your technology, or they may see opportunities in working together on joint projects to improve cost or performance. By researching customer requirements, you can identify other opportunities to build stronger relationships.

Independent research can supplement the information on your database and provides the most objective form of information to make key account decisions. There are other ways in which you can obtain this information:

● Telephone research into customer satisfaction with a recent purchase – what were the most important factors in selecting the equipment?

● Telephone research into future buying requirements – what would you look for in selecting your next product?

● Analysis of recent competitive purchases of products and services – what combination of support services and products is the customer buying and what does this tell you about their requirements?

- Published surveys of industry buying patterns. These can provide background information to the independent commissioned research, but the quality of the information depends on the willingness of leading companies to participate.

This research into customer requirements helps to answer the question – would closer relationships help customers meet their most important requirements and, more importantly, can you meet those requirements?

ASSESSING COMPETITIVE THREATS

Although you may recognise opportunities to grow or protect your business by building closer relationships with your customers, you may not always be in the driving seat. You may be forced into partnership by competitive action but you must be sure that the account provides you with competitive benefits as well as protection. Your database and your market research should provide you with information on competitive activity and you can use this as a basis for analyzing opportunities:

- Who are your main competitors?

- What percentage of potential key account business do they hold?

- How long have they been dealing with the customer?

- How do your products compare with competitive offerings?

- What are your competitors' main strengths?

- Have they invested in links with customers which would make it difficult for other suppliers to make inroads?

- Have you got the skills and resources to overcome the competitive threat?

- Are any competitors making inroads into businesses where you are currently the dominant supplier?

- How do your competitors compare with the customer requirements identified in the last section?

- What are customers' attitudes towards your competitors?

- How do they compare with attitudes towards your company?

Competitive analysis helps you to identify how you can protect your most important business and, more positively, how you can strengthen your position with customers in situations where your competitors are currently holding a larger share of the business than you. To strengthen your position with a customer where competitive activity is growing, you must be certain that the investment is positive. If you build stronger links with a customer, is the customer's business growing in line with your investment? If your investment simply maintains the business at a static level, you may be missing other opportunities. If the actions you take to protect your business provide you with new opportunities, there is a strong basis for partnership.

Increasing the level of technical support you provide to your customers may enable you to strengthen your links with the technical department and raise your profile within the organization. A higher technical profile could provide you with new business opportunities that were not previously available. In the same way, improvements in your own design or manufacturing processes to drive down costs or increase value for money may increase your own efficiency or provide you with the capacity to handle additional products for your key customers.

Competitive analysis should be utilized at two levels:

- Will the actions you take protect your existing business against competition?

- Will the actions also provide additional business opportunities?

ANALYZING CUSTOMER ATTITUDES

It is also important to understand customers' attitudes towards your company and towards your competitors. If your customers believe that you have the capability and the resources for strategic supplier status, there may be a firm basis for success but, if research shows that customers hold a particular view of your company compared with your competitors, the opportunities may be more limited. You have a choice of either risking failure in your initial moves or undertaking an action programme to improve perceptions in areas that are important to partnership.

By understanding your customers' attitudes to your company and to your competitors, you can make effective decisions about the potential of partnership opportunities and improve your chances of winning those opportunities.

Customers regard market understanding as an important factor in assessing strategic suppliers. This understanding is not just important for impressing potential customers, it also helps you assess the opportunities for partnership. By analyzing your customers' performance in the marketplace, you can identify their strengths and weaknesses and put forward proposals that will enable them to improve their competitive performance. Recording customer information from sources such as corporate brochures, annual reports and press information on your database will help you to build an understanding of your customers' current achievements. You should also integrate information from published industry surveys and research material which shows how your customers are perceived in relation to their competitors and how they meet the main requirements of their marketplace.

The information will help you to build a picture of your customers' position in the market:

- What are their main markets?

- Are their markets shrinking or growing?

- What are your customers' positions in the marketplace?

- How have their positions changed over the last five years?

- Who are your customers' main competitors?

- How are they regarded in the marketplace and how have their relative positions changed over the past five years?

- What are their key success factors in the market?

- What are the long-term trends in the market?

- What new technical developments will be needed to succeed in the market?

- Could innovation help your customers to succeed?

- Do your customers need to improve their quality standards or their delivery performance?

- Are your customers aiming at market leadership or an increase in share?

- Are new international market opportunities likely to be available?

- Are your customers considering entry into new markets?

● Do you have skills that are relevant to the new market?

Making this information available on the database will help your sales and marketing staff demonstrate this understanding and show how you can help your customers achieve their objectives.

UNDERSTANDING CUSTOMER STRATEGIES

It is equally important to understand your customers' business strategies – what is their corporate direction, how do they aim to succeed, what are their key objectives? By aligning your objectives with theirs and showing how your products or services can help them to achieve their strategic business objectives, you demonstrate that you can make an important contribution to their business. The analysis of customer strategies will help you to develop a number of scenarios for partnership:

● Your customers want to achieve market leadership through innovation. Your technical skills and resources can help them develop the right level of innovation without investment in their own skills.

● Your customers want to become value-for-money suppliers and succeed through competitive pricing. You can help them reduce overall costs by improving design and manufacturing costs or by handling non-core activities cost effectively.

● Your customers want to increase their capacity so that they can compete effectively with larger competitors. You can supplement their resources by providing external skills and resources.

● Your customers want to rationalize their operations to concentrate on their core business. They can utilize your specialist skills to supplement their resources and allow their key staff to focus on strategic business tasks.

● Your customers want to maintain their market position by strengthening their supply position. You can provide them with a quality-assured source of supply that provides them with continuity.

This series of scenarios shows that an understanding of your customers' strategic objectives can provide you with an opportunity to build strong relationships that increase your customers' dependence on you.

As the previous section showed, products and services that help your customers to meet their strategic business objectives can increase customer dependence. The more your customers depend on you, the stronger the opportunities for partnership. Use your database to see if any of the following scenarios apply:

- You are the only supplier of a key component that is vital to your customers.

- Your main competitor has gone out of business and your customer now has only a single source of supply.

- Your customer must develop new products quickly to retain and protect market share and your products are critical to their product development programme.

- Your customers have to reduce their cost base to compete effectively and your processes and services will help them to succeed.

- Your customers need to improve their levels of customer satisfaction and your products and services are vital to their success.

Identifying opportunities like this requires a detailed understanding of the customer's business and a close working relationship that allows you to focus on their problems and opportunities.

the forces behind partnership

Partnership does not happen in isolation; nor do buyers and sellers suddenly decide to change the nature of their relationship. Partnership occurs because there are initiatives from either supplier or buyer driven by a need to improve a company's competitive performance. These driving forces include:

- Increasing competition in the marketplace.

- Higher customer expectations.

- Pressure on costs.

- Rapid technological change.

- Need for rapid new product development.

- Skills shortages.

- Introduction of new business processes.

INCREASING COMPETITION Companies are facing increasing competition from many different sources.

- *Low-cost competitors, particularly from developing economies.* Quality is acceptable, in many cases good, but the competitors are operating from a low-cost base or taking advantage of new technology or government support to reduce their start-up costs. Examples include the bearing and fastener industries where the Japanese and East Europeans concentrated a low-cost, high-volume attack on European industry; consumer electronics; and cars. Although the "new suppliers" have now matured, in many cases other new competitors are emerging using the same techniques.

FAST TRACK

Does your database include information on competitive activity at each of your main accounts. By analyzing the main competitive threats, you can identify priorities and plan a suitable response.

- *Speciality competitors – companies which concentrate on a narrow, often high-volume sector of the market.* By using available technology and avoiding the cost of supporting a wide range of products, these companies are winning a significant share of the market and damaging their established competitors' customer base. Examples include book printers, particularly in the high quality "coffee table" sector; personal computers; and speciality clothes outlets such as ties, socks and jeans.

- *Competitors who add value to their products to win volume business, segment markets or who offer packages of products and services that represent better overall value.* Examples include insurance companies; computer manufacturers which "bundle" software with their systems; car manufacturers which include service and rescue packages; and energy companies which include consultancy and management services in their overall offering.

- *Competitors who come from a different discipline but utilize their customer base or their physical location to attack established suppliers.* Examples include petrol outlets moving into the convenience store business; banks offering mortgages and insurance services; building societies offering banking services; and management consultancies offering information systems services.

MEETING CUSTOMER EXPECTATIONS

In many cases, competitive activities are driven by increasing customer expectations. New car buyers, for example, expect to receive satisfactory service throughout the ownership of the car. The finance package, the after-care programme, the accessories and services such as mobile communications, the convenience of guaranteed rescue services and the benefits of a single source for all motoring services such as bodyshop, repairs, windscreens, spare parts and customization all put considerable pressure on the resources of a typical local car dealer.

FAST TRACK

What does the database tell you about customers' preferences? Have any new products had a significant impact on their purchasing patterns?

The travelling public expects to buy more than petrol, oil or roadmaps when they call at a service station anywhere in the country. To sustain a high quality, consistent retail service across a national network of local outlets changes the nature of fuel station management. Industrial buyers expect a range of support services such as consultancy, implementation and maintenance when they buy capital equipment. Customers who are commissioning complex projects such as new buildings want to simplify their own administration and management tasks by dealing with a small number of suppliers or preferably a single source.

Distributors, retailers and agents expect their suppliers to provide them with a full support package to help them develop their own business. In each of these scenarios, customers expect a standard of service that goes beyond the basic product. The supplier is unlikely to have the skills and resources to provide these additional services without recruiting, retraining or investment. Partnership offers the opportunity to develop these additional services, meet customer expectations and achieve increasingly higher levels of customer satisfaction.

PRESSURE ON COSTS

Price competition and the need to maintain profitability are increasing pressure on every company to reduce its cost base. Since the recession, companies cannot afford to be complacent about pricing and companies are looking at every aspect of their operations to see where they can reduce costs. In industry, cost reduction not only applies to the cost of bought-in materials and the manufacturing process, it can also be applied to the following areas:

- Distribution.
- Warehousing.
- Stockholding.
- Quality control on incoming components.
- Administering the supply chain.
- Design and engineering processes.
- Through-life costs of the product.
- Operating internal or external support services.
- Recruiting and training staff.
- New product development..
- Marketing and selling.
- Achieving customer satisfaction.

FAST TRACK

Database marketing allows you to categorize the key cost factors that influence the success of partnership and use these to plan communications programmes and identify cross-selling opportunities.

○ *What are the key elements of your customers' cost base?*

○ *Which "cost reduction" activities would have the greatest impact on different customers?*

As the examples in this chapter showed, partnership can make an important contribution in each of these areas. Cost reduction is one of the primary reasons behind partnership. In its simplest form, a supplying partner is offered a larger share of the customer's business over a longer period of time in return for agreed price levels maintained over that period of time.

The customer then has a better and more predictable cost base, while the supplier enjoys higher levels of business with reduced sales and marketing costs. A more advanced form of partnership sees both companies co-operating on joint cost-reduction exercises, for example by modifying production processes, increasing quality to reduce waste or reworking, or achieving savings through re-design or value engineering of key components.

RAPID TECHNOLOGICAL CHANGE New technology can reduce costs, improve reliability and product performance and increase customer satisfaction. The problem is that technology changes rapidly and few companies have the resources to achieve technical leadership without major investment in research and development and recruitment of high quality technical staff. Increasingly, they rely on the specialized technical expertise of their suppliers to contribute developments in specific areas.

FAST TRACK

○ *Looking at sales of your own products on the database, what group of products do your customers see as innovative?*

○ *How quick is the uptake of new products?*

Take a car for example. Technical changes could occur in a large number of unrelated areas, but few of them would be developed by the car manufacturer's own technical staff. Here are just some examples:

● Better tyre design to improve road holding and comfort.

● Improved seating design to improve comfort and safety.

● Lighter and stronger materials to reduce overall weight and increase safety.

● More sophisticated braking systems to improve safety.

These technical improvements are likely to come from an external supplier although the impetus may come from the car manufacturer. The car manufacturer would not have the technical resources to achieve industry-best standards in all of these areas. Yet, to remain competitive, it must have access to the technology. Partnership with suppliers who have a record of innovation will provide that access. Partnership not only provides access to specialist technology, it may also provide a manufacturer with a specific competitive edge. By developing new products and services that are unique to the partnership, a customer can develop technical advantage over competitors and secure the advantage for a sufficiently long period to build an effective marketing lead.

By maintaining information on industry trends on your database, you will better placed to take advantage of new opportunities.

DEALING WITH SKILLS SHORTAGES

One of the other pressures driving companies is the shortage of skills in key areas such as design, engineering or marketing. Skills shortages mean that staff can be prevented from taking on strategic development tasks because of the pressures of day-to-day working. In companies that have made a large investment in information systems equipment from a number of different sources, there is now a drive to integrate different products so that they operate together and enable companies to improve the competitive advantage they obtain from their investment. Systems integration, however, is just one of the pressures on information systems support staff. They have to train new users, develop new business applications, support and maintain systems and manage relationships with information systems suppliers.

The cost of recruiting and retaining staff of the calibre to handle all of these tasks effectively can be prohibitive and, therefore, outsourcing appears to be the only viable alternative. However, outsourcing without deep involvement in the customer's business can lead to ineffective service, so partnership offers an attractive solution.

FAST TRACK

○ *Do your customers buy "people" services and does this indicate that they have skills shortages?*

○ *How does the purchase of services compare with the purchase of products?*

Outsourcing can be used to overcome short and long-term skills shortages and deal with peaks and troughs in the workload. Using the computerization example again, the implementation of a new departmental system could take a number of months from initial consultation and system development through installation and start-up. Each of the stages would require different skills and different levels of involvement from support staff. The company would have to retain or redeploy staff to meet short-term requirements and this would not represent the best use of resources.

INTRODUCTION OF NEW BUSINESS PROCESSES

Re-engineering and core business development are just two of the new business processes that companies are utilizing to improve their competitive performance. Total Quality Management, Just-In-Time Manufacturing, World Class Manufacturing and many other approaches to business have each provided the manufacturer with a new way to manage the business. Partnership integrates with each of these processes to provide companies with high levels of flexibility and the opportunity to take advantage of advances in manufacturing technology.

FAST TRACK

○ *Have you captured information about changes in your customers' business processes?*

○ *Will they require new skills to help them succeed?*

Just-In-Time, for example, aims to reduce overall costs by squeezing waste out of the supply system. Manufacturers do not hold buffer stocks, they only hold stocks to meet specific production requirements. Suppliers, in turn, produce sufficient quantities to meet current requirements. The Just-In-Time process depends on high levels of co-operation between manufacturer and supplier and partnership in the natural business relationship. Information and communications systems which enable partners to exchange product information, plan production and delivery and retrieve information on work-in-progress strengthens the business and physical links between partners. The high levels of co-operation needed to ensure efficient operation by both parties can only operate in a partnership environment.

Total Quality Management, at its logical conclusion, demands integrated quality processes throughout the supply chain, and partnership is often the logical outcome of a drive to improve quality standards. By harmonizing quality standards, a manufacturer can reduce the cost of monitoring incoming supplies and ensure quality in his own products.

DON'T FORGET!

Partnership initiatives can come from suppliers or customers, and they can be led by other developments in management practice. At the heart of all the driving forces, however, is the need to improve competitive business performance and, whenever this can be achieved with mutual benefit to both parties, there is a real opportunity for partnership. By analyzing the purchasing patterns of major customers and utilizing research data on customer attitudes and requirements, it is possible to identify and meet those expectations.

6

improving customer service standards

This chapter looks at ways in which you can utilize information on a database to improve standards of customer service. The contribution of a database can be as simple as providing basic customer information to speed up call handling or as complex as an expert system that allows faults and problems to be diagnosed quickly. The key to quality customer service is building comprehensive information and making it available to the people who deliver the service.

improving response to customer requests

Technology and a customer database can be used to improve the quality of customer service by making it easier and quicker for companies to respond to customer requests. A call reception centre, for example, which co-ordinates all the incoming service calls enables a company to manage the quality of its telephone response. Technology alone cannot improve the quality of service, technology plus the right people, training and customer information is a powerful combination.

EXAMPLE

Making the connection

The ICL Connection is a good example of a call response strategy which makes full use of the power of technology to deliver service. The Connection uses telecommunications technology to link customers anywhere in the UK with specialists anywhere in the UK and represents a major investment in training and technology. A comprehensive database on all customer information and service history is held in a central location, but is accessible to anyone in the company who needs to use the information. ○

**THE KEY TO GOOD
SERVICE**

● Provide customers with a 24-hour response service to maintain high levels of customer loyalty. This reassures customers that they have the full support and backing of a professional organisation. The database provides the information for a quality response whenever the customer calls.

● Use technology to provide customers with a diagnostic and monitoring service. This provides round-the-clock peace of mind that their equipment is in secure hands. Security companies, for example, provide remote control centres that monitor the status of their customers' security systems and take immediate action to deal with faults or incidents. A database that holds complete service history provides an excellent starting point for a rapid response.

● Develop software to help individual equipment users deal with routine maintenance and simple faults quickly without having to make service requests. Information from the main service database can be analyzed to identify the most frequent queries and these will form the basis of the customer software.

These examples of technology are now in common use, but companies have assessed them from the point of view of service performance, rather than customer service benefits. The key benefit is reassurance and a quality response to customer service requirements. To identify opportunities for marketing this type of service, it is important to identify the service requirements of a broad range of customers and prospects. The database provides information for that.

when this approach is suitable

Use your customer database to identify customers who fall into the following "high-risk" categories. Quality service will be important to them and you should target them with information on your service offering.

DEPENDENT ON RELIABLE EQUIPMENT OPERATION
Business customers may depend on continued reliable operation of their equipment to maintain their competitive business performance and a rapid, quality response to service requests is vital. For example, a bank cash dispensing system must be constantly available and any faults dealt with quickly. The technology exists to monitor equipment condition and predict service requirements before faults occur; companies supplying high-value equipment can take advantage of sophisticated monitoring equipment to improve performance and reliability. The right standard of service ensures that customers are able to operate their own business efficiently and deliver high standards of service to their own customers.

CRITICAL REQUESTS
Customers expect an immediate response to critical requests. Motoring organizations, for example, know that customers who have broken down need reassurance and accurate information on the support they will receive. The motoring organizations have invested in communications technology that enables them to accurately pinpoint the location of breakdowns and respond quickly with help. Response like this builds high levels of customer satisfaction by improving convenience. The database is used to record members' details and control the company's service resources. Customer databases can be invaluable in helping customer service staff quickly provide advice and guidance to

customers over the phone. A service operation, for example, should hold complete service records of all customers' equipment, together with customer information. Any customer request can be quickly compared with information on the database as a basis for a prompt response.

a customer service strategy

DON'T FORGET!

ICL developed its customer response strategy to take advantage of customer database information and the power of communications. Database information enabled it to identify prime prospects for each type of service and refine their service offerings by asking questions such as "How many customers require 24-hour cover, how many customers have external maintenance contracts?"

The company supplies mainframe and departmental computers to customers throughout Europe and provides them with a full range of support services from initial consultancy through to maintenance. Services are important to customers because they ensure that their equipment continues to operate reliably and provide business benefit.

To provide a national service to its customers throughout the UK, ICL had a network of local branches, each providing service to a defined group of customers. As in most branch networks, the larger branches had greater resources to provide service which meant that there was inconsistency throughout the network. With each branch holding its own customer database, it was difficult to get an overall picture of service requirements.

The key to success for ICL was a combination of technology and customer care. Technology would enable it to offer a more sophisticated service that was consistent across its customer base, but this had to be balanced with high standards of personal service from all staff so that the customers received the highest levels of care. There were a number of important aspects to the customer response strategy:

- Centralisation of customer response through a national call reception centre which replaced calls to local branches.

- Development of a customer response service which was monitored to independent quality standards.

- The introduction of centres of excellence for fault diagnosis and customer support, providing consistent support to customers nationwide.

- The use of a sophisticated service database which maintained customer equipment information and provided comprehensive fault diagnosis information.

- The introduction of communications systems for field engineers that enabled them to access the database for support when they were working on the customer's site.

WATCH OUT!

ICL understood that technology alone would not provide the right level of service, so it carried out a company-wide customer care training programme which ensured that all staff were customer focused.

NATIONAL CALL RECEPTION CENTRE

The Connection was the name given to ICL's purpose-built call reception centre. Instead of dialling local branch numbers and obtaining local service, the customer could now dial a single number and have immediate access to any specialist within ICL. The calls were routed over the network and charged to the customers at local rates so that there was no cost penalty for using the new national service.

The Connection was available 24 hours a day throughout the year and was designed from the outset as a single reference point for all customer requests. Customers could:

- Report faults.

- Request service visits.

- Ask for telephone advice and guidance.

- Request literature or register a complaint.

All of these requests were logged on the central customer database as a basis for analyzing service performance and developing service packages to suit the needs of individual customers.

Offering a single point of contact simplified the process of obtaining information or support and got round the problem of asking the customer to phone another extension or another number. In many cases, the call receptionist was able to deal with the customer call immediately – logging a request, dealing with a query or providing information. However, where the call required the support of specialists, the receptionist took details of the call and co-ordinated the call-back process. The call receptionist would route the call to the appropriate specialist and then call back the customer to advise on the way the request would be handled. The call receptionist would then monitor progress on the response and keep the customer up-to-date with progress.

Don't just use your database as a source of information for efficient customer handling, use it to monitor response and service performance. The result – customers are kept fully informed.

FAST TRACK

CENTRES OF EXCELLENCE

The key to providing a consistent standard of service was the introduction of centres of excellence. Here product and technical specialists were concentrated in groups with access to a central database to provide a high standard of service to all customers. Specialists were able to carry out diagnosis over the telephone or work with an engineer on site by providing telephone support. The approach did not replace the traditional engineers on site; it simply made them more effective and freed them for more productive work. It also ensured the most appropriate type of engineer dealt with the fault and the correct spares were available to complete the job.

The service database was an integral part of the centres of excellence. ICL collated world-wide information on the performance of its systems to build up profiles of the faults and queries that were most frequent. This provided a number of important benefits:

● It allowed the specialists to provide a rapid response to routine service queries by comparing symptoms with the information on the database.

- It allowed ICL to identify the most common service requests and to provide information to customers which would eventually reduce the number of routine requests.

- It enabled ICL to develop customer support software that would allow customers to deal with simple service requirements themselves.

- The database also helped call receptionists and support specialists to gather preliminary detailed information on the customer's equipment and service history without wasting the customer's time answering routine questions.

COMMUNICATIONS FOR SITE ENGINEERS

The database was also a valuable form of support for engineers working on customer sites. They were provided with specially-developed hand-held terminals which provided them with two-way access to the service database. The engineers were able to obtain diagnostic information which enabled them to complete the task quickly and they were also able to update the customer's service records immediately. The customer could feel confident that work would be carried out efficiently to the highest standards.

dealing with customer incidents

If you deal with incidents, how much do you know about the incidents and the people using the services? What levels of service are most appropriate? A database can help you quickly identify the right type of response.

Customers who know that their problems are taken care of will be fully satisfied with the services that are available and will be happy to deal with the same company in the future. Quality experts have found that a key factor in delivering time-guaranteed services is the ability to reassure customers that help is on the way. Customers are then prepared to wait until help or support arrives even if there is a long gap between reporting the incident and having it resolved.

So, if vital manufacturing equipment breaks down, the equipment supplier could offer a 24-hour, 4-hour or 1-hour call-out service. Customers, as the research showed, are not too concerned how long the repair would take provided they were kept informed.

FAST TRACK

Recording customer attitudes on your database and comparing competitive offerings are a valuable starting point in developing a customer response strategy.

○ *How long should a service call take?*

○ *What level of cover should be provided?*

○ *How should support requests be handled?*

○ *What happens if the incident is not resolved within an agreed timescale?*

AN INCIDENT MANAGEMENT DATABASE

The incident management approach is to appoint one person, trained in customer service skills to deal with a customer throughout an incident – reassuring the customer, providing advice and guidance, co-ordinating the support services and keeping the customer informed on progress. For the incident manager to be fully effective, it is essential that all customer and incident information is immediately available via a database.

Incident management can be applied to any service-led organization where the customer needs to be kept informed – maintenance and support services on vital equipment for example or disaster recovery services where the customer faces many difficult and unfamiliar decisions, and needs constant support to reassure them.

Lost travellers cheques

EXAMPLE

Companies which provide travellers cheques offer their customers a 24-hour helpline anywhere in the world to get financial help or advice on their holiday money. Lost cheques or exchange problems can be handled efficiently with minimum disruption to the holiday giving the customer peace of mind and increasing customer satisfaction. ○

Insurance helplines

EXAMPLE

Insurance companies offer their customers helplines for motoring cases or domestic problems. The customer can call, get immediate support services, plus advice on how to proceed and make a claim. The same principle of re-assurance applies. During an incident, the customer can be uncertain of how to proceed and welcomes advice and guidance to minimize distress and inconvenience. ○

IDENTIFYING OPPORTUNITIES FOR INCIDENT MANAGEMENT

It is important to identify situations where support like this is valuable. The database enables you to build a profile of the type of customers as a basis for direct marketing. Typically these might include:

- Where the customer could suffer a great deal of inconvenience and stress as a result of the incident – reducing the stress and inconvenience helps to demonstrate high levels of care and increase customer satisfaction.

- Where the incident threatens the company's efficiency, measures must be taken to limit the damage.

- Where the customer does not have the skills and resources to resolve the problems on the spot and is dependent on external forms of support.

Incident management at the RAC

EXAMPLE

Incident management approach is used as part of a number of motoring packages offered by the RAC. The packages are grouped together under the heading "assured mobility" and are offered direct to private motorists, branded as a fleet service or part of a car manufacturer's drivers' package. The overall package includes the following elements:

○ Roadside, home and rescue services for simple repairs.

○ Recovery of the vehicle to the customer's next destination or home.

○ Alternative methods of onward transport for the customer, including contribution to the cost of public transport, hire car or hotel costs for overnight accommodation.

The Personal Incident Manager takes responsibility for these services and reassures the customer that help and support are on the way. Information on the database also allows the Personal Incident Manager to offer a range of other related services that help the customer. These include:

○ Making hotel, hire car or hotel bookings on behalf of the customer and arranging settlement.

○ Informing family or business colleagues on the customer's behalf.

○ Offering legal advice if necessary.

This compares favourably with all the problems a customer might face if they had to co-ordinate all the support activities themselves. The Personal Incident Manager approach aims to reduce the "hassle" in an incident and allow the customer to get on with their normal business. ○

- Where the customer has paid for a support package and has agreed to a certain level of response, the company must respond within the agreed levels.

- Where the speed of response is seen as a competitive differentiator and is positioned as an integral part of the service package.

- Where failure to deal with the incident quickly could have a critical effect on the customer's business or personal activities.

- Where the incident could have legal implications and the customer needs high levels of advice and guidance.

SETTING OBJECTIVES FOR INCIDENT MANAGEMENT

In developing a database to support your response strategy, you can ensure:

- The highest levels of customer support during an incident.

- Minimal inconvenience for the customer.

- Prompt resolution of incidents within agreed timescales.

- Quality response and support throughout an incident.

- Effective deployment of support resources, maximizing customer satisfaction.

OPERATING AN INCIDENT MANAGEMENT PROGRAMME

The database is key to the success of incident management. It allows the incident manager to deal promptly with the customer, identify the skills and resources needed and monitor the process of response. The database information is also valuable to the marketing team. It enables them to identify recurring fault patterns and customer needs as a means of fine-tuning the service.

making it easier to do business

Developing a customer database and providing sales staff with online access to the information can make it easier for customers to buy from you. Many companies put up artificial barriers to trade by making their ordering procedures complex, failing to provide adequate product information or setting up complex procedures for billing.

The key is the database. By integrating customer information, sales order processing and production control systems, sales staff are able to provide the customer with up-to-date information and simplify ordering.

Cutting the paperwork at ICI

EXAMPLE

When ICI was assessing the benefits of electronic payments systems, it estimated that it was raising vast amounts of paperwork with thousands of suppliers. This exercise would have kept a large purchasing department fully occupied and prevented the purchasing staff from carrying out anything more than basic operations. However, by utilizing an electronics payment system, it was able to reduce the paperwork mountain and ensure that purchasing staff were able to concentrate on improving supplier performance. ○

Customer scheduling at Ford

EXAMPLE

Recent developments in business process re-engineering show that it is possible to improve this process still further. Ford Trucks worked in partnership with key components suppliers to develop a system that put the onus on the suppliers to decide when they should deliver components. The suppliers were able to access Ford's manufacturing schedules to plan their own production schedules. The logical outcome of the process is here where the supplier acts as an internal department supplying to requirements, rather than responding to ad-hoc requests. The purchaser does not have to raise paperwork or even plan schedules – that is taken care of by the supplier. ○

ONLINE ORDERING Ordering costs both supplier and purchaser money, so anything that can simplify the ordering process will save your customers money and improve customer relationships. With the growth in computerized manufacturing and stock control systems, companies are using online ordering to simplify administration. A motor dealership with a number of regional branches used online ordering to speed up and simplify its parts ordering procedures. Branch staff were able to access the central parts database over public communications networks; they could get immediate information on the stock available of various parts and place their orders. Stock levels were automatically adjusted and the system produced delivery notes, invoices and picking instructions. This process cut out several layers of paperwork and speeded up ordering and delivery.

The online ordering process can be extended to key customers with its logical conclusion in the Ford system described earlier. Online systems depend on high levels of information and effective communications links between supplier and buyer; although detailed guidelines are outside the scope of this book, companies can either set up their own dedicated networks or utilize public networks.

Just-In-Time (JIT) is a process of meeting customer delivery and stock-holding requirements by integrating planning, communications and distribution. Customers can reduce their own stockholding levels and maintain adequate cover for their product requirements because suppliers plan their own production levels and distribution levels in line with customer requirements. When customers need stock, it is delivered, literally, just in time. JIT depends on close co-operation between supplier and customer and utilizes computerized production control systems to exchange information that is used for planning.

FAST TRACK

If you operate a split-ordering system, the database can help you identify changing patterns of business:

○ *Are customers ordering more frequently?*

○ *Has the value of the orders changed?*

○ *Has the total order value increased?*

Simplifying customer access can improve customer convenience. By creating a company-wide database and a central contact point for all customer enquiries, you can ensure that every incoming customer contact is handled efficiently. This is particularly appropriate for companies who have a number of separate locations or who are organized by product group. At the national enquiry centre, all incoming calls are handled by a central reception centre and routed to the appropriate specialist. The customer does not have to waste time trying to track down the right contact. The centre should handle incoming calls for queries such as:

- Product information.

- Technical information.

- Service requests.

- Literature.

- Complaints.

- Estimates and ordering.

- Delivery.

- Accounts.

By recording and analyzing different types of requests via a database, it is possible to determine information needs and plan a communications strategy.

DON'T FORGET!

Making it easier for your customers to buy is a sure way of improving customer satisfaction. Electronic ordering and payments systems, for example, can reduce mountains of paperwork. Communications also make it easier for your key customers to obtain up-to-date commercial and delivery information and lay the foundation for processes such as Just-In-Time which enable you to build even stronger customer links. Providing your customers with a single point of access for all enquiries makes it easier for them to do business and allows you to control the quality of customer contact.

By incorporating this type of information into the database and analyzing the requirements and ordering patterns of individual customers, it is possible to enhance customer service and improve customer satisfaction.

7

improving direct marketing performance

This chapter looks at the role and benefits of direct marketing, the activity that is most closely associated with database marketing. It describes the scope of direct marketing and shows how the database can be used to improve the performance of this precise medium.

the scope of direct marketing

Direct marketing includes the well-established techniques of direct mail and mail order, as well as increasingly popular techniques such as telemarketing, direct response advertising and relationship marketing which are covered in other chapters. Direct marketing depends on a quality database to enhance sales and marketing programmes. It:

- Gives you more flexible options for marketing.

- Provides a cost-effective alternative to other forms of advertising.

- Enables you to reach specific sectors of your market with precise, targeted communications.

- Provides a cost-effective alternative to retailing and other forms of distribution.

- Reinforces the effectiveness of other marketing activities such as advertising and personal selling.

setting direct marketing objectives

Precision is the essence of direct marketing and objectives should therefore be measurable However, these general objectives should be translated into precise, measurable objectives such as:

- Raise awareness of our product range amongst 35% of technical directors in the mechanical engineering sector.

- Ensure that purchasing managers in our 10 top customers are contacted at least once a fortnight.

The more precise your objectives, the more effective your campaign will be. Success can be measured in a number of ways:

- Measuring the response rate to a campaign.

- Tracking the number of resulting leads or sales on the database.

- Tracking changes in purchasing patterns resulting from the campaign.

achieving direct marketing objectives

BUILDING DIRECT SALES

This objective is important if:

- Customers can only buy direct from you.

- You wish to supplement or replace your retail network.

- You want to sell to niche markets that can only be reached by direct marketing.

- The products can be sold through direct marketing, ie they do not have to be inspected by the customer or demonstrated.

EXAMPLE

Office product sales

An office products manufacturer could no longer afford to maintain a direct salesforce calling on office equipment retailers and major customers. However, the customer database provided the basis for a mailing list. The manufacturer mailed a quarterly catalogue to all customers and set up a telemarketing operation to take orders and maintain contact with customers. By segmenting the database he was able to develop special versions of the catalogue for schools and local government. Selected large customers were mailed regularly with special offers and the response is tracked on the database. ○

EXAMPLE

Limited edition products

A manufacturer of limited edition products has monitored cost of sales through different channels. Direct response advertisements in quality Sunday newspapers provided valuable leads and database information. The database generated a list of established customers who received privileged advance mailings of future product offers. ○

Retailers' direct catalogues

EXAMPLE

An increasing number of retailers publish catalogues of either popular lines or special editions. The products are identified by analyzing product purchasing patterns and the target audience is selected using purchasing history and profiling. The catalogues are mailed to customers or offered to prospects through advertising or direct mail. Catalogue customers are able to order products directly for home delivery. Retailers can increase customer loyalty and increase geographical coverage without opening new branches. ○

GENERATING SALES LEADS

This objective is important if:

● You depend on a direct salesforce or you use agents, distributors or retailers to handle local marketing.

● You are entering new market sectors where you do not have an established customer base.

● You have a large number of lapsed customers on file.

Offer consultancy or demonstration

FAST TRACK

Use your database to identify key prospects who may be difficult to reach. Prospects are mailed product or service information with an invitation to take advantage of a demonstration or consultancy. The database information is used by the telemarketing team to handle incoming enquiries or follow up written responses. This technique can also be used to reach "hidden" decision-makers who respond to a targeted offer.

FAST TRACK

Lapsed customer marketing

Use the database to generate a lapsed customer file. These customers are mailed or phoned with an update on the company's latest products and services. The salesforce is then given the task of converting them to live customers. The database can also be used to record reasons why customers have been lost as a basis for corrective action.

SUPPORTING SALESFORCE ACTIVITY

Direct marketing is an integral element in improving salesforce performance. It can be used to overcome a number of problems where:

- The salesforce cannot reach important decision-makers.

- The salesforce does not have the resources or the time to maintain regular contact with decision-makers.

- The salesforce does not have the time to follow up good leads quickly.

- The salesforce does not have the skills to present complex arguments.

EXAMPLE

Customer contact strategy

A computer manufacturer wanted to maintain regular contact with senior decision-makers. However, between major system sales there was little opportunity for salesforce contact. The manufacturer identified key decision-makers from the database and established a quarterly contact strategy. They were mailed a series of management guides which formed part of the manual and offered discounts on other useful sources of information. The mailings added value to the relationship and maintained high profile contact between salesforce visits. By setting up a contact "diary" on the database they were able to make better use of salesforce time. ○

IMPROVING THE EFFECTIVENESS OF OTHER FORMS OF COMMUNICATION

If your marketing budget is split between different communications activities such as advertising, sales promotion and publications, it is essential that each activity works as effectively as possible.

EXAMPLE

Integrating campaigns

Three computer software suppliers reported that they had integrated their advertising, direct mail and telemarketing operations. Prospects who replied to advertisements were mailed with a series of software offers. Selected prospects were also followed up by telephone. Responses to the mail-shot averaged around 3%. However, when the suppliers added telemarketing, response rates grew dramatically to 12, 15 and 18% respectively. The database was used to compare the effects of different campaigns and offers. ○

EXAMPLE

Sector mailings

A professional services company produced a corporate brochure which described its capability and its services. However, research into customer preferences showed that service requirements varied by market sector. These preferences were recorded on the database and used to plan communications with individual sectors. The company did not have the budget to produce different versions of the brochure so it built sector-specific messages into a series of mail-shots which accompanied the brochure. As a follow-up to the brochure, prospects were mailed sector-specific case studies at regular intervals. ○

RAISING AWARENESS

Raising awareness of a company, product or service is important if:

● Your company is entering new markets where you do not have an established reputation.

● You are launching new products which appeal to specific sectors of your market.

● You are trying to influence important decision-makers who may not be aware of your company.

EXAMPLE

Seminar invitation

A company moving into a new market sector wanted to demonstrate its capability and its potential contribution to new prospects. Its existing database only held limited information on the new sector so, to improve understanding and raise awareness in the market, the company sponsored a seminar at which recognized consultants reviewed new developments in the market. The seminar also included exhibitions where the company was able to demonstrate its products. The seminar invitations were mailed by the company. This helped to introduce the company to important prospects and demonstrated that it intended to become a key player in the market. Prospects who replied to the invitation were added to the company's database and followed up with regular mailings. ○

MAINTAINING EFFECTIVE CONTACT

This objective is important if:

- There is a long gap between product purchases and you need to maintain customer loyalty.

- You sell low-value products in a very competitive market and brand loyalty is low.

- You are dealing with a customer whose decision-making process is complex and negotiations are spread over a long period.

- Customers buy at frequent intervals, but your competitors are very active.

EXAMPLE

Customer magazine

A components manufacturer with a large customer database produced a quarterly magazine which was mailed to all customers. The magazine included features on new products, customer-facing staff and improvements in service. The magazine also included special reader offers and information on social events that helped to improve customer loyalty. To enhance the information on the database, readers received special offers and the response helped to highlight their preferences. ○

Case histories

EXAMPLE

A marketing consultancy had targeted a group of blue-chip companies as prime prospects, but was aware that it might take as long as a year to win a contract as an approved supplier. Although personal contact was likely to be the most effective form of communication, the consultancy found it difficult to maintain regular personal contact. Analysis of potential direct sales costs also indicated that direct contact could prove expensive. The consultancy planned a series of regular monthly mailings utilizing case histories that were relevant to the prospect's business. These helped to show how the consultancy operated and proved useful to the prospect. ○

BUILDING RELATIONSHIPS

The stronger your relationship with your customers, the more opportunities you have to influence the future direction and success of your business. Relationship marketing is important if:

● Your company depends on a few key customers for the majority of its business.

● Your customers want to rationalize the number of suppliers and you want to remain on the approved list.

● You have an opportunity to improve customer loyalty by building long-term relationships with your customers.

Customer clubs

EXAMPLE

An automotive refinishing manufacturer wanted to build stronger long-term relationships with bodyshops and distributors. The company set up a customer club which offered customers privileged discounts, regular special offers, social events and a high level of business support. Club members received regular information bulletins and participated in long-term incentive programmes. The club enabled the company to develop close relationships with customers and to increase levels of repeat purchase. The database was used to generate prospects for the club and to track the changes in expenditure that were attributable to the club. ○

operating a direct marketing campaign

The database can help you plan and manage direct marketing campaigns. It can be used in:

- Defining the target market.

- Planning the timing of the campaign.

- Deciding the frequency of the campaign.

- Measuring response.

- Evaluating different approaches.

DEFINING THE TARGET MARKET   Do you want to reach all customers and prospects, or are you targeting specific groups of customers and prospects? Direct marketing is a precise medium, so your campaign could be aimed at just one key decision-maker or thousands of potential users. To plan your direct marketing campaign, you should use your database to analyse your target market.

TRICKS OF THE TRADE

The more information you have about your target audience, the more precise you can make your campaign. In an ideal world, direct marketing would allow you to communicate on a one-to-one basis with every prospect but, in practical terms, you are more likely to be communicating with groups who share the same characteristics.

- Who buys your type of product?

- Who influences the purchasing decision?

- In business buying, who are the important decision-makers?

- How many potential buyers are there?

- How many users are currently buying your product and what is your share of the market?

- How many prospects do you want to reach with the direct marketing campaign?

- Where are the prospects located?

- Do you need to communicate with the actual buyers or with other people who influence the purchasing decision?

- What are the characteristics of these people – age, sex, income, job title?

- What are their most important considerations in choosing a brand or a supplier?

- What does available research tell you about their attitude towards your company and your products?

- How do they currently get information about your products?

- What is the role of direct marketing in reaching the target audience?

CAMPAIGN TIMING

With direct marketing, you do not have to consider advertisement publication dates, the campaign can run at any time. However, timing may be dictated by other factors – lead times for producing mailing material, seasonal purchasing patterns, product availability, tender dates.

These are some of the factors to consider in planning the timing of your campaign:

- When is your customer making the buying decisions?

- Is there a formal contract tendering schedule?

- Does the product have a seasonal purchasing pattern?

- Do you know when your customers hold product/purchasing review meetings?

- Do you know when your customers' financial year ends?

- If you are launching a new product, when will the product be available?

- Does your direct marketing campaign have to tie in with the timing of any other marketing activity – an exhibition, advertising campaign or salesforce call?

- Are there any holiday or quiet times that should be avoided?

- When will you be able to follow up the campaign?

DECIDING CAMPAIGN FREQUENCY

A single mail-shot, telephone call or direct response advertisement may produce results, but a series of quality contacts will have greater impact and ensure you meet your objectives. Multiple direct marketing activities provide a number of benefits:

- Raise levels of awareness with each contact.

- Follow up contacts who have not responded.

- Move individual respondents further along the decision-making process.

- Maintain contact during extended decision-making processes.

The database can help you to plan campaign frequency by analyzing the results of previous campaigns.

- What is the purchasing frequency of the product?

- Which campaign frequency was most effective in increasing sales?

MEASURING RESPONSE

The database should be used to measure the response to direct marketing activities. However, it is important to establish what actions you want your prospects to take:

- Place an order.

- Request a sales call.

- Request further information.

You can then compare the cost and performance of different response options such as:

- Postal-based response mechanisms:
  - Reply-paid cards
  - Reply-paid envelopes
  - FreePost addresses.

- Telephone-based response mechanisms:

  - FreePhone 0800 which is free

  - Lo-call 0345 numbers which only cost callers local rates

  - 0891 numbers which cost a specified amount.

- Fax-based mechanisms

  - Freefax 0800 which is free

  - FastFax services which provide specified product information at normal call rates.

EVALUATING DIFFERENT APPROACHES

Part of the flexibility of direct marketing is that you can test your approach before committing resources to the full campaign. The database allows you to measure and compare the response to a number of different elements, including:

- The offer.

- The creative approach.

- The target audience.

- The response mechanism.

- Frequency and timing.

- Integration with other communications programmes.

The test campaign can be carried out in a number of ways:

- On a representative sample of the target market.

- In a defined sales or geographical territory.

- To a particular sector of the target market.

The most effective test campaign is the one that achieves the highest response levels.

the mailing list

This section provides guidelines on creating and using the most important element in a direct marketing programme – the list. In its simplest form the list simply includes names, addresses, job titles and telephone numbers of customers and prospects. However, the basic list can be refined by adding information on buying patterns, lifestyle and many other factors to provide a comprehensive picture of customers and prospects.

This section explains how to develop lists from your database and other internal sources, and how to obtain and use external lists.

INTERNAL SOURCES OF INFORMATION

You can use internal sources to compile a database of both customers and prospects suitable for mailing. The most important sources are:

- Customer records.
- Customer correspondence, including records of complaints.
- Warranty records.
- Service records.
- Sales prospect files.
- Salesforce reports.
- Records of lapsed customers.
- Market research surveys commissioned by your company.
- Business information library (if your company has one).

TRICKS OF THE TRADE

Customer records on your database are probably your most valuable asset as they invariably generate the highest response rates when they are mailed with relevant information.

Customer records can quickly provide you with names and addresses of individuals but, to get more specific information that enables you to segment your list, you will have to carry out further analysis. Simple segmentation of your database might give you categories such as:

- Customers who have bought in the last six months.

- Lapsed customers.

- Customers who spend over £** per annum.

Depending on the information available, the same type of analysis can be applied to your prospect lists.

Internal database information is probably the most economical way to build a mailing list – the information is already available and you do not incur the costs of renting standard lists or researching new lists.

WATCH OUT!

However, there are several disadvantages:

○ *The information may not be in the form you need.*

○ *The information on a particular market or sector may not be comprehensive.*

○ *The information may be out of date.*

○ *Your internal lists may limit you from expanding the market for your products.*

If your internal sources do not provide sufficient information to compile a comprehensive mailing list, you should consider using external information sources to fill the gaps or expand your internal lists, renting ready-made lists from external suppliers or commissioning specific lists from external suppliers.

EXTERNAL SOURCES OF INFORMATION

If you want to compile your own lists, you can use a number of external sources to supplement internal information. External sources include:

- Directories:

- general trade directories

- trade directories for specific industries

- membership directories for associations and groups

- local telephone or chamber of commerce directories.

- Magazines and newspapers:

    - specialist magazines and yearbooks

    - recruitment sections of newspapers

    - business reports and industry surveys in daily/weekly newspapers.

- Published surveys:

    - industry surveys

    - summaries or reports on consumer surveys.

- Government and industry statistics:

    - census

    - industry reports

    - trade association statistics.

- Public information services:

    - databases and information services available via public networks.

You can use this external information in two ways – to provide you with names and addresses of additional prospects or to provide you with an understanding of market developments so that you obtain additional names and addresses that match these developments.

USING EXTERNAL LISTS If your database does not provide sufficient information to compile your own lists or if you are moving into new markets where you have no information, you may be able to make use of existing lists. Lists are available from a number of different sources, including:

- List brokers who offer different categories of lists.

- Magazine publishers who offer lists of their readers.

- Directory publishers.

- Trade associations or professional institutes which offer lists of their members.

- Commercial organizations which offer lists of their customers.

- Retailers who offer lists of their account customers.

Many of these lists are advertised in marketing and direct marketing magazines, although some list owners may not publicize their activities and you may have to approach them directly. For example, a non-competitive commercial organization with a customer profile similar to your own may not have considered external use of its own list.

WATCH OUT!

In selecting a ready-made list, you should check a number of factors:

○ *How closely does the list match your customer profile?*

○ *How much wastage will there be in the list, ie how much of the list falls outside your customer profile?*

○ *Are there any product or service restrictions on use of the list? The owner may wish to protect the customers against direct mail "overload", or may wish to maintain an air of exclusivity.*

COMMISSIONING LISTS

Standard lists may not give you the degree of match you need and you may wish to commission a special tailored list that matches your requirements exactly. The successful preparation of a tailored list is directly related to the quality of the brief and you should provide the supplier with a detailed description of your target audience. Your brief should include the following information:

- Who buys your type of product?

- Who influences the purchasing decision?

- In business buying, who are the important decision-makers?

- How many potential buyers are there?

- Where are the prospects located?

- What are the characteristics of these people – age, sex, income, job title?

Compiling a tailored list like this may require a joint effort between market research specialists, database management specialists and direct marketing agencies which handle data capture and database management.

ADDING TO YOUR LISTS

Many of the standard lists and the lists you have compiled yourself from internal or external sources may not match your requirements exactly. To improve coverage or to make them more precise, you need to make a continuous effort to refine them.

WATCH OUT!

○ *Ensure that new customer and prospect data is added to the list.*

○ *Include coupons and other reply mechanisms with every form of communication and add the responses to your lists.*

○ *Encourage the salesforce to provide up-to-date customer and prospect information.*

○ *Maintain an active search programme in appropriate magazines and newspapers to identify new prospects for your list.*

SEGMENTING YOUR MAILING LISTS

A basic list contains names and addresses, telephone numbers and job titles in business lists. A list as simple as this allows you to carry out direct marketing only in the most general sense. The strength of direct marketing is that it can provide a high degree of precision. To take advantage of that precision, your lists must be structured carefully.

CONSUMER LISTS

● Marital status.

● Income level.

● Occupation category.

● Homeowner/home value.

● Car owner/car value.

● Personal interests.

● Credit card holder.

- Shopping patterns.

- Holiday preferences.

- Insurance status.

- Leisure interests.

- Brand preferences.

- Recent purchase history.

- Reading/viewing habits.

BUSINESS LISTS

- Type of business.

- Size of business

- Number of employees.

- Annual expenditure.

- Average order size.

- Purchasing frequency.

- Head office/local purchasing.

- Purchasing history.

- Key contacts.

- Job title.

- Budget authority.

This information can help to reduce the waste in a direct marketing campaign and ensure that the offer accurately reflects the prospect's needs.

USING POST-CODING   Location can be an important factor in planning a direct marketing campaign. Regional variations in purchasing patterns may be strong enough to justify regional campaigns. A company may not have the resources to market its products nationally and decides to concentrate on regional markets. The direct marketing campaign may be integrated with advertising or promotions in selected regional markets.

One of the simplest methods of operating a regional campaign is to utilize the post-code. The post-code structure allows more and more precise geographical segmentation.

- There are currently 120 *post-code areas*, represented by the first one or two letters of the postcode.

- There are currently 2,700 *post-code districts*, represented by the figure in the first half of the postcode.

- There are currently 8,900 *post-code sectors*, designated by the figure that begins the second part of the code.

- Below the level of *post-code sectors*, there are individual addresses which are represented by the final letters in the code.

A post-code list can be used at a very simple level to reach all prospects in a given post-code area, district or sector. While this may be perfectly adequate for regional business campaigns, it may not be precise enough for more sophisticated consumer campaigns. Post-code information can be supplemented with geodemographical or lifestyle information to provide a more precise form of targeting. Two of the most important categories of information are:

- ACORN (A Classification of Residential Neighbourhoods) which enables companies to select districts or sectors that most closely reflect their own consumer profiles.

- LIFESTYLE profiles which rank sectors according to marketing criteria.

Post-coding is essential to ensuring accurate, rapid delivery of direct mail campaigns but it can also be used as the basis of highly targeted marketing campaigns. Royal Mail Streamline, for example, offers companies the Household Delivery service which delivers unaddressed mail according to the customer's requirements. A product with broad consumer appeal could be mailed to all addresses or selected *post-code areas*, while other mailings can be targeted on *districts or sectors* that match the consumer profile. A service like this can reduce the costs of compiling and managing lists, and the costs of addressing individual mailshots. If your lists do not have post-codes, you can have them added by a computer bureau approved by the Royal Mail.

If the database or mailing list holds complete names and other information, direct mail letters can be personalized in a number of ways:

● *including the name in the address and greeting only* – Dear Mr Jones

● *including the name throughout the text* – ... and Mr Jones you'll be glad to know that you've won a special prize ...

● *including other customer information throughout the text* – we hope the Mondeo you bought from Anytown Motors last month is giving you miles of trouble-free motoring.

Information such as this can be handled by most word processing packages using a mail merge function. The main text of the letter is held in a primary file with commands to indicate where the customer specific information is to be inserted. Customer information is held in secondary files or address files; the information is divided into fields such as name, address, post-code, greeting, customer-specific messages or paragraphs.

The personalized letters can then be printed to resemble individually typed documents using laser printers or inkjet printers.

a powerful, flexible, precise medium

For an organization with a diverse marketing programme, direct marketing can prove to be an important element. As the name implies, direct marketing is a precise medium, enabling organizations to communicate directly with key segments of their market. An industrial company with a small group of key customers, each with different characteristics, can communicate on a one-to-one basis with each account. A consumer goods company that uses broadcast techniques to reach a mass market can add highly-targeted follow-up to customers who respond to the initial advertisement.

The increasing sophistication of database marketing techniques means that companies can now build more detailed profiles of markets, market segments and individual customers. By analyzing purchasing histories and other data on purchasing patterns, companies can assess their customers' propensity to buy and develop targeted campaigns that will move them towards purchase and build long-term relationships.

This adds considerable control and flexibility to the marketing process, minimizing the potential waste in broadcast techniques. For organizations with limited budgets, direct marketing can prove to be an extremely cost-effective medium. Marketing communications can be focused on key customers and prospects, while the performance of the campaign can be precisely measured.

Direct marketing also forms an important element in an integrated campaign where it can add to the effectiveness of advertising, public relations and other communications activities. An advertising campaign that includes a response mechanism can be followed up, first by direct marketing and then by telemarketing to increase conversion rates.

Direct marketing forms an important part of customer relationship programmes where it allows an organization to plan a long-term contact strategy that recognizes the specific communications needs of individual customers. Organizations in the financial services sector, for example, recognize that they have an opportunity to build relationships with customers for life. Banks, in particular, are aware that customers rarely change a current account, yet they have not exploited the fact by offering them portfolios of services to meet changing needs. Direct marketing would put customers on a campaign track and ensure that the contact strategy reflected their changing needs.

DON'T
FORGET!

Direct marketing is one of the most versatile communications media in both business-to-business and consumer markets. It can be used in its own right as a precise powerful medium and it can also be used to support other sales and marketing activities. Direct marketing allows companies to target their message precisely, change them to suit different market requirements and operate both tactical and strategic campaigns without the restrictions of advertising production and publishing lead times.

8

effective telemarketing

This chapter looks at the growing importance of telemarketing and explains how the database can be used to improve the effective handling of both incoming and outgoing calls. Telecommunications technology is likely to transform this activity even further, but the technology itself will not deliver quality service. The right information and personal skills are essential.

the competitive edge

Effective communication is vital to corporate survival and success and the telephone is becoming the most important part of the communications strategy. In many areas, it is replacing post and personal contact as the most efficient way to send, receive and process information. The combination of database information and effective telemarketing techniques can help to develop a powerful competitive edge. Many companies now recognize that telemarketing can help them make the most effective use of the telephone – increasing revenue, reducing costs and improving customer service.

Although telephone technology is advancing rapidly and sophisticated telemarketing systems are available for small, medium and large businesses, companies are still reluctant to take advantage of the marketing opportunities.

TRENDS IN TELEMARKETING

- 34% of marketers have a dedicated inbound telemarketing team, compared with 45% in sales and customer service.

- 29% of marketers have a dedicated outbound telemarketing team, compared with 35% in sales and customer service.

- By the year 2000, inbound calls are likely to exceed 400 million per annum, a fivefold increase in current levels.

- 12% of UK packaged goods companies now offer their customers a helpline service compared with 43% in the US.

BT's Business News quotes research that shows people are increasingly keen on buying by phone. 67–80% of those interviewed claimed they found telephone ordering easy and convenient. Telephone ordering is used successfully in a wide variety of industries, including computer hardware and software, car insurance, office stationery components and catalogue-based products.

The telephone is probably the most important interface between your organization and your customers. It is vital for increasing sales, taking orders, handling enquiries, delivering customer service or collecting payments. Here is how two leading companies are using telemarketing.

EXAMPLE

Freemans

Freemans is the UK's most successful mail order company. It has a turnover of £650 million and 16% of the UK mail order market. 90% of its orders are taken by telephone and each call represents £70-£100 income. Convenient ordering is key to the process. Customers want to get through quickly and know that orders will be fulfilled quickly and accurately. The order lines are open 24 hours a day and take around 300,000 orders a week. The company has two order centres and uses network services to switch calls for the most efficient handling. Customers are provided with Lo-Call rates and offered price incentives for telephone ordering. ○

EXAMPLE

The Rover Group

The Rover Group used outbound telemarketing to contact small fleet operators to generate leads for dealers. In one campaign, 120,000 calls resulted in sales of 3,000 cars worth over £2 million. The information was also used to update the customer database reducing waste levels in mail canvassing. ○

the importance of the telemarketing database

Telemarketing offers considerable business benefits but the database is crucial to success. It has three main roles:

1 To provide customer information to operators so that they can improve customer handling.

2 To provide a basis for proactive selling to the customer.

3 To help gather and use additional customer information via the telephone.

At minimum, a telemarketing database should contain the following information:

- Name.
- Address.
- Account number.
- Purchase history.
- Preferences/special requirements.
- Products and services bought.
- Frequency of purchase.
- Contact history.

The operator has all the key information to hand whether it is an outbound sales call or an inbound call handling orders or enquiries. By linking telephones and computers, for example, staff can handle calls quickly and efficiently and provide a highly personalized service. With Computer Telephony Integration (CTI), calls can be co-ordinated with computer-based business applications. Information screens can be automatically generated as a call is answered and both calls and screens can be transferred simultaneously. This improves both productivity and customer service.

CTI can also be used to generate outgoing calls automatically and intelligently, again with screen information. This can increase the productivity and efficiency of telemarketing staff, particularly in intensive outbound applications.

**TRICKS OF
THE TRADE**

The right software can help to improve customer service and productivity:

○ *Linking telephones and computer information screens can reduce the time taken to handle queries or provide quotes.*

○ *One financial services company increased its call handling capacity by 300% by utilising the right software.*

The key benefit of information on a customer database is improved customer handling. Here is an example of a dialogue between a customer and a receptionist who is making good use of the information on the database.

Garage   Good morning, Mr Jones, how is the GTi? Has it been running okay since we tuned it last month?

Customer   Yes, it's been its old self again. I was actually calling about the brakes. I think they might need attention.

Garage   You're probably right, we check them on the regular service, but the last time we changed the pads was two years ago and you've done more than 25,000 miles since then. We'll have a look at those for you.

Customer   When can you do it?

Garage   I'll book it in for tomorrow, brakes are a priority job. Actually, I've just looked at your service record, you're due for an interim service in three weeks. Would you like us to do that while the car is in? It would save you coming back again later.

When a regular customer calls you to place an order or service request, how do your staff respond? Do they waste the customer's time asking for basic details or do they make the customer feel important by having all the information to hand?

If we look at that scenario again, here are the key processes:

- Ask the customer for a unique identifier – name, registration/serial number, customer number.

- If possible, put the caller through to a named receptionist who has dealt with the customer before.

- Make sure the receptionist has access to full service information, ideally on a database.

- Take the opportunity to offer other services while the customer is having work carried out.

- Make it as convenient as possible for the customer to have work carried out.

Effective reception works in any business. It makes the customer feel welcome, demonstrates commitment to customer service and provides the opportunity to add value and increase business.

PROACTIVE SELLING TO THE CUSTOMER As the script showed, telemarketing staff with access to a good customer database can take the opportunity to offer additional products or services to their customers, provided they are relevant. The receptionist in the example knew the customer's car service history and was able to highlight work that would actually need to be done.

As the following examples show, the database can provide valuable support:

PROMPT   By identifying past purchasing patterns, the database shows the customer is willing to buy certain types of product.

ACTION   Remind customers that they have not bought recently and point out that they can easily order over the telephone.

PROMPT   By identifying purchasing frequency, the database shows when a customer is next likely to buy.

ACTION   Remind customers that they usually buy the product about this time and offer to take an order.

PROMPT   By building profiles and comparing customer data, the database highlights likely prospects for a specific type of product.

ACTION   Suggest to the customer that although they have not bought this type of product before, you feel it may be of interest and offer to send them more details.

PROMPT   By grouping related products by type of customer, the database can highlight opportunities for sales of complementary products or services.

ACTION   Suggest to the customer that if they are buying product A, they may also need product B or service C at the same time. Offer them information or take an order.

Two examples from the travel industry show how this process works.

A highly-targeted offer

The more you know about your customers, the better you can serve them. Although the package holiday accounts for an extremely high proportion of holidays, database information is increasingly used to offer customized holiday offers to individuals. A recent advertisement for a frequent flyer programme demonstrated the potential of database information to customize the offer and strengthen customer relationships. The company is able to target the customer so precisely because it has been gathering information on flying patterns and choices and using the database to build a profile of individual customers. Armed with this information, the telesales operator can make a very targeted offer and build customer loyalty:

● This man flies with us regularly on business.

● He took a family holiday in Spain during the Barcelona Olympics.

● His last flight to Munich was during the World Athletic Championships.

● The promise of a free family ticket to Sydney should keep him loyal to us.

Selling related services

Airline reservation systems, which are used to automate the process of booking, can also be used for highly effective telemarketing. When a customer books a flight to a particular destination, the system can prompt the telephone operator to offer a whole range of travel-related services specific to the customer's destination, including:

● Accommodation at "partner hotels".

● Car hire from the airport.

● Onward public transport from the airport to the customer's destination.

● Reservations at a social or sports event that coincides with the customer's visit.

If the customer is a regular traveller, the telesales operation can become even more personalized. Here's how the discussion might go:

> 'Shall we book you into the usual hotel and hire a car for you?'
> 'By the way, there's a great ballet on the week you're there. Shall we book tickets for you?'

GATHERING ADDITIONAL CUSTOMER INFORMATION

Many companies are using the information generated through telemarketing to build databases as the basis of direct marketing programmes. They use them to carry out a variety of marketing tasks such as:

● Sending special interest catalogues to different market segments.

● Identifying high spending customers.

● Developing product strategies.

● Offering loyalty incentives to high spending customers.

TRICKS OF THE TRADE

Woolwich Building Society experienced a 150% increase in response rate by including a FreePhone number. Norwich Union believes that people provide more information when they call in, than when they complete coupons.

Helplines can be one of the most useful ways of finding out about customer needs and obtaining information on individual customers.

If you've been through the traumas of buying a personal computer, you'll understand the problems of trying to choose from hundreds of "me too" products, each one claiming to offer the ultimate solution to your needs. If you then tried to work out which of the manufacturers' extensive hardware/software packages was right for you, you'll understand why customers sometimes need help in choosing a product. In providing that help, don't forget to gather and record information about the customer. Here's how the helpline works.

- The FreePhone facility encourages people to use the service and discuss their requirements at length.

- The helplines are manned by specialists who combine technical knowledge with an ability to talk to individuals at the right level – callers are not intimidated by talking to people who reply in jargon.

- Helpline staff talk about the customer's needs – how they plan to use the computer, what results they want, how often they use it. They concentrate on identifying the customer's needs, not doing a sales pitch on their products.

- Staff are encouraged to develop a relationship over the phone, not deal with queries as quickly as possible and meet a daily target. Dialogue and a relaxed attitude help to build customer confidence.

The customer who gets honest, straightforward answers will trust the company. The company offering the helpline service gets a detailed profile of individual customers.

So, don't just reserve helplines for operating problems or service requests. Use them to build a relationship before the selling starts. Once you have established customer needs, your sales team can concentrate on offering the right product. The result – customer satisfaction at every stage and the basis for some highly-targeted marketing.

FAST TRACK

Telemarketing can provide valuable data so it is vital that this information is utilized.

○ *Set up links between telemarketing and main marketing databases to transfer data.*

○ *Set up remote links to your database if you are using an external agency to handle telemarketing.*

building more advanced telemarketing operations

THE CALL CENTRE
SOLUTION The combination of modern telecommunications techniques and database marketing is powerful. Smaller companies can use a basic telephone system and part-time telemarketing staff, but companies who want to go further should talk to their telecommunications suppliers about "Call Centre" solutions.

Call Centres improve the way both incoming and outgoing calls are handled. By linking telephones and computers, for example, staff can handle calls quickly and efficiently and provide a highly personalized service. By adding automated services, your telephone-based business operations can be extended to 24 hours a day at no extra cost. This can improve convenience for callers and allow you to provide a more flexible service.

Call Centres can lower your operating costs, increase the opportunity for generating revenue, increase management control and improve customer service.

EXAMPLE

The UK's leading paging operator, Hutchison Paging, uses a CSL Call Centre solution to answer 4000 calls per hour. 98% of calls are answered within eight seconds and only two callers in every thousand hang up before the call is answered. ○

Multiple technologies can now be blended into single business applications to meet your individual requirements. Each Call Centre can be designed to incorporate one or more of the following elements.

Automatic Call Distribution (ACD) allows high volumes of incoming calls to be queued and routed to waiting or specified agents. This ensures that calls are answered in sequence and no calls go unanswered.

With Computer Telephony Integration (CTI), calls can be co-ordinated with computer-based business applications. Information screens can be automatically generated as a call is answered and both calls and screens can be transferred simultaneously. This improves both productivity and customer service.

CTI can also be used to generate outgoing calls automatically and intelligently, again with screen information. This can increase the productivity and efficiency of Call Centre staff, particularly in intensive outbound applications.

Interactive Voice Response (IVR) allows callers to access your computer systems directly to place orders, modify data or request standard information. No operator is required and this can significantly improve productivity and flexibility in handling routine enquiries and transactions.

Frequently-requested information can be stored on fax and sent automatically on request. Fax confirmation of orders or other details can be generated in real time and sent directly from the Call Centre system. This also improves productivity and flexibility in handling routine calls.

Voice-based bulletin boards can be used to provide pre-recorded routine information automatically.

With *voice messaging*, callers can leave messages for later response if no staff are available when they call. The call back function can be automated if appropriate to maximize efficiency and customer service.

Electronic mail can be used to generate any written follow-up to an incoming call.

MANAGING CALL CENTRE OPERATIONS

Effective performance measurement is essential to efficient Call Centre management as a basis for optimizing customer service and staffing levels. Reports and statistics are available on telephony data, number of calls answered or lost and average speed of answer. Management systems can also link Call Centre data to other business statistics such as numbers of orders taken or average order value. This can help to measure the real contribution of the Call Centre to the business.

EXAMPLE

Shorrock Limited

Shorrock Limited, the leading UK security company, used a Call Centre with IVR to double staff productivity. Service engineers can now access Shorrock's computer system directly from any standard telephone line. The company was able to double its business without any increase in telephone staff. ○

You may already have a Call Centre in your organization but, if not, look closely at your business to see if there are opportunities to improve the speed and quality of call response. Call Centres are widely used in finance and banking, utilities, transport, entertainment, reservations and catalogue shopping. Increasingly, competition is encouraging other businesses to see how they could use Call Centres to improve the performance of activities such as:

- Enquiry and help desks.

- Telemarketing.

- Retail or wholesale order entry.

- Reservation systems.

- Customer service departments

EXAMPLE

Coopers and Lybrand

Coopers and Lybrand implemented a Call Centre to improve the service available from its IT help desk. IVR now allows 50% of calls to be handled automatically, while CTI and ACD ensure that callers who do need personal attention are answered quickly and efficiently. ○

profiting from customer calls

According to the marketing director of a mail order company, the telephone is proving to be a vital element in quality customer service. If your business receives a high volume of incoming calls – sales, information or service queries, bookings or transaction processing – you need to ensure that those calls are answered quickly and efficiently. A quality response not only enhances customer service, it is the key to increased revenue and profit.

If you make it easy for customers to contact you, you'll soon develop closer relationships but, put barriers in their way, and they'll just try the next number on their list.

Developments in telecommunications technology mean that sophisticated response systems are no longer the preserve of large corporations. Systems are now available to small and medium sized businesses that can transform the quality of customer response. The key is Call Centres.

By concentrating your telephone specialists in Call Centres, supervising their performance, and using a technique known as Automatic Call Distribution (ACD), you can ensure that calls are answered quickly and efficiently, with the optimum use of staff time and telephone lines.

A small engineering company invested in a Call Centre system to handle sales order processing and provide customers with a technical helpline service. Although it had offered telephone support in the past, the service had been hampered by poor call-handling techniques. At peak times, customers would wait several minutes to get through and were sometimes transferred to extensions that were unmanned. The customer's perception was shaped by the call responce not by the service that was eventually delivered.

The system they installed uses a range of computerized tools to monitor performance and improve control over call response. Information on the status of telephone lines and groups of Call Centre staff shows what is happening to calls as they come in and allows the supervisor to manage operations efficiently. The system also includes features such as call queuing and call prioritization to ensure that the Call Centre operates cost-effectively and delivers high levels of customer satisfaction.

The engineering company found that the system allowed it to handle the same volume of calls more efficiently but, more importantly, it could keep customers informed even while they were waiting. User-friendly queuing techniques are used to ensure that calls are answered in sequence and no calls go unanswered. All incoming calls are queued and answered in order and the system can be programmed to feed calls to waiting or specified agents automatically:

- Calls are automatically routed to the longest waiting agent in a group.

- If all agents in a group are busy, calls can overflow to a second group.

- Calls can be routed to other groups after a preset ringing time.

A range of call processing options can be utilized to enhance call response even further:

- Integral call sequencing reduces the risk that callers will hang up by giving an informative message.

- Voice Mail allows callers to leave messages for agents who are unavailable.

- Automated Attendant answers calls automatically and transfers them to the right extension.

- Integrated Voice Response (IVR) order processing system answers callers automatically and takes details without agent intervention.

You may already have a Call Centre in your organization but, if not, look closely at your business to see if there are opportunities to improve the speed and quality of call response. Call Centres are particularly appropriate for the following activities:

- Enquiry and help desks.

- Telemarketing.

- Financial services.

- Retail or wholesale order entry.

- Reservation systems.

- Customer service departments.

By monitoring the length of time it takes for incoming calls to be answered and assessing the workload on different members of staff, you can plan a Call Centre that meets your business needs. These are some of the important factors to consider:

- What type of calls should the centre handle – orders, enquiries, help, service?

- Should it be a central facility or based in different regions?

- What is the target call response time – how long can you keep callers waiting?

- How many staff and how many lines will be needed to handle planned volumes within the target response times?

Networking facilities allow multi-site companies to operate a single Call Centre; customers call their local branch, but the call is re-directed automatically to the Call Centre. A distributed Call Centre network means that callers can overflow to remote sites in peak periods or be diverted to specialist centres of excellence in different sites.

These network options increase flexibility and can be used to enhance customer service even further. Many systems allow you to link computer and business applications to your telephone operations. For example, the integration of screen-based customer information can help to improve productivity and customer service on call response. To maximize the benefits of the Call Centre, agents can make outbound sales calls or enquiries when incoming traffic is low. For increased productivity, outbound calls can be generated from a database with integrated call information available on screen.

Although the use of call handling systems is not new, the technology is now more accessible and it is being increasingly used by small and medium sized organizations in the public and private sector. It can provide the basis for a highly efficient telephone-based customer contact system and research shows that effective contact is a key factor in achieving the highest levels of customer satisfaction.

making the most of telemarketing

TELEMARKETING AND ORDER TAKING

- Make sure your database has basic customer information so that you don't waste customers' time.

- Offer FreePhone and Lo-Call numbers make it economical and simple for customers to place orders quickly.

- Use the database to speed up response times and improve levels of customer service.

- Order takers can be trained to increase sales by building rapport with customers; the database should provide them with all the customer information they need.

TELEMARKETING AND CUSTOMER SERVICE

Telemarketing can improve the quality of customer service:

- FreePhone and Lo-Call numbers can encourage customers to keep in touch to ask for information or to complain.

- Record customer queries or complaints on the database is a way of enhancing understanding of customer needs.

- Identify any customer concerns on the database.

- Use a technical help service to free up the field technical force and provide a rapid response to service calls.

TELEMARKETING AND SALES FOLLOW UP

Telemarketing can be used to follow up sales enquiries and other sales leads. The calls can take a number of forms:

- Call the prospect to obtain further details for the database.

- Offer information on products and services generated through profiling.

- Make a promotional offer that is shown on the database to be effective for that sector.

TELEMARKETING AND DIRECT SALES

Telemarketing supports a direct sales operation through planned calls to customers and prospects. The calls can take a number of forms:

● By analyzing the customer's purchasing history, you can call to stock levels and offer customers prompt delivery.

● Use relevant promotional offers as an incentive to buy immediately.

● Update customers and prospects on price and availability.

DON'T FORGET!

Telemarketing in conjunction with an effective database marketing operation can improve your sales, marketing and customer service. However, it must be used properly. Some recent research shows that performance can be poor, despite advances in technology:

○ *Response to inbound sales calls is currently very patchy:*

– *20% of callers have to try the number more than once*

– *20% of calls have to be transferred*

– *Transfer delays can be as long as 30 seconds*

– *26% of callers wait an average of 48 seconds while the salesperson finds information.*

○ *65% of callers said they would take their business elsewhere if the call was unsuccessful.*

9

sales promotion

This chapter looks at the way database techniques can improve the effectiveness and contribution of sales promotion. Traditionally, sales promotions have been used as short-term tactical tools, with no attempt to gather customer information. Increasingly, both retailers and manufacturers are recognizing the value of promotions in providing customer data and contributing to long-term relationships.

role of sales promotion

Sales promotion plays an important role in marketing a company's products and services. It can be used for a variety of different strategic and tactical marketing tasks, including:

- Obtaining sales leads.

- Encouraging prospects to try a product or service.

- Persuading customers and prospects to switch brands.

- Increasing customer or retailer loyalty.

- Helping to develop the image of a product or service.

- Improving retail performance.

In a number of cases, sales promotion can make a contribution to increasing long-term sales volume, enabling manufacturers to reduce the unit cost of the product. Sales promotion is unlikely to impact on marketing performance if there are significant product differentiators, for example if a product has a much higher level of features than a competitor or if there is a large price differential. Sales promotion is at its most effective when products are similar in price and performance.

EXAMPLE

Thomas Cook

Thomas Cook operates in a fiercely competitive marketplace. The company strengthened its marketing activities with a database marketing programme supplemented with data captured at the point of sale and lifestyle information. The database provides such information as spending power, whether customers travel alone or with families, special interests, when they book and frequency of repeat purchasing. Data can then be segmented to produce targeted promotions that reflect the special interests of travellers. For example, personalized cruise offers, ski holidays, or holidays linked to sporting events. The company can also use the database to cross-sell other services such as hotels, car hire, foreign exchange. The database plays an important role in promoting products and services, and it also plays a valuable role in supporting other campaigns. ○

---

generating information from sales promotion programmes

Card-based collector programmes that yield customer information are more valuable than traditional systems. Simple collector schemes simply encourage purchase and yield no information. However, card schemes that allow customers to collect points encourage loyalty and repeat purchase. The information can then be used to develop segmented mailings and track purchasing patterns, while the most sophisticated systems allow cross-selling and the development of long-term customer relationships.

EXAMPLE

British Airways

In 1993, BA flew around 26 million passengers. Of those, were around 750,000 business travellers who are crucial to BA's success. They are the frequent flyers who form the majority of the one million plus Executive Club database. The key to success is keeping in touch with those customers between flights. The use of special airport lounges and Air Miles are two of the most important tools. The membership card provides all the important information for database marketing – favourite seats, smoker or non-smoker, dietary, flying patterns and spend. This means that any marketing activity can be highly targeted. The card enables BA to segment its database into three main categories from high-paying passengers to economy class frequent flyers.

The Dream Ticket promotion was based on that understanding – passengers were offered a flight to any one of 350 destinations. By paying the full fare one way they could earn enough Air Miles to cover the cost of the return flight. Many members of the Executive Club had accumulated enough Air Miles to select some of the more exotic locations so they were able to see a direct return for their loyalty. ○

protecting brands with database promotions

Branded products are suffering attacks on all fronts, principally from own label products, the strength of retailers and the increasing importance of media such as direct response television. They can no longer assume that mass marketing techniques will be wholly successful and they can't guarantee that success on one product in the range will be repeated on range extensions. The brand needs to be marketed more consistently across all media otherwise, with the proliferation of media and markets, customer loyalty is irrelevant. Research also showed that consumers were finding it difficult to distinguish between brands in terms of product performance and therefore they had to find other ways to add value to their relationship with the consumer. Database marketing therefore provides a powerful method of building brand loyalty.

EXAMPLE

Buitoni

Food manufacturer, Buitoni, had already used direct marketing successfully. It used direct response advertising to capture data through the offer of an Italian cookbook. Consumers on the database were then invited to join a club with the promise of a regular newsletter on Italian cooking, travel and lifestyle. Club members are mailed with regular special offers which are segmented to reflect their specific interests.○

---

cross promotion of products

Cross promotion allows complementary products to be promoted in a cost-effective way. The database can be used to identify opportunities for cross promotion:

● Identify the profile for a product.

● Look for products with a similar profile.

Cross promotion of Sony products

EXAMPLE

Sony has a range of complementary entertainment and information products – both hardware and software that can be used for cross promotion:

○ Compact discs and cassettes offered as on-pack promotional items

○ Buy 100 computer diskettes and get free Walkman.

assessing the effectiveness of promotional programmes

● How do you justify spending money on promotions?

● What return on your promotional investment are you looking for?

● What are the related sales objectives?

● How will you quantify them?

Database techniques allow you to:

● Measure and compare the response to different offers.

● Categorize prospects who respond to promotions.

● Track resulting sales.

● Capture data on customers.

● Utilize data for direct marketing.

● Isolate the effect of non-promotional activities.

● Assess the promotional impact across your business.

● Identify significant account, sector or regional differences in impact.

● Decide whether the differences relate to techniques, premiums, value, customer appeal or communications.

● Profile people who used previous promotions as a basis for planning.

improving sales promotion performance

OBTAINING SALES LEADS

Sales promotion can be used to support the direct sales process by providing sales leads or encouraging prospects to arrange a sales meeting. It works in conjunction with direct response advertising and other forms of direct marketing to provide information for a prospect database. There are a number of potential approaches:

- Offer an incentive for responding to an advertisement, such as entry in a competition or a free gift.

- Offer an incentive for direct purchase via the advertisement, for example a special price or special offer for orders placed by a specific date.

- Invite readers to book a sales appointment, with the offer of free advice or guidance, or a free gift.

In each case, the respondent provides valuable sales data in return for a special offer. The use of targeted incentives can increase the level or quality of response, so it is important to use the database to assess the effectiveness of different types of incentive.

Increase response levels

An insurance company wants to increase the number of enquiries as a means of growing its life assurance business. Advertisements in the national press include a response coupon which features an incentive to reply, such as "Simply return the coupon and we'll send you a superb fountain pen, free".

Database Action
To determine the right incentive, try a number of different offers and measure the response to each.

Target specific prospects

A speciality clothing retailer wants to attract potentially high-spending subscribers to a new direct sales catalogue. Advertisements in prestige magazines offer respondents discounts on expensive country house weekend breaks as an incentive for ordering a catalogue. The company is targeting consumers with the right level of spending power for their products.

Database Action
Use database information to segment your prospect lists. Measure the response to different types of offer.

Shorten the response cycle
A food manufacturer wants to run a direct marketing campaign for a seasonal product. To ensure that it has an up-to- date database available in time, it runs a promotional campaign offering free recipe booklets to respondents who reply within seven days of the offer.

Database Action
To obtain information quickly, include a simple response mechanism and follow up with telemarketing to obtain further data.

Book a meeting
An engineering company wants to increase the number of appointments so that its sales team can present a new product to customers and prospects. The company mails an incomplete gift to prospects with the offer of the missing component for people who arrange meetings. The promotion increases the number of bookings and reflects the engineering company's advertising theme – "the missing link".

Database Action
Use sales records to identify accounts where it is difficult to obtain appointments.

ENCOURAGING PROSPECTS TO TRY A PRODUCT OR SERVICE
Getting customers and prospects to try a new product or service is an important stage in the marketing process. It is essential to the success of the following marketing activities:

● Operating a pilot trial for a new product.

● Launching a new product.

● Launching an existing product into a new market.

● Extending a product range.

Sales promotion can be used to obtain a high level of trials and there are a number of potential approaches:

- Offer a free sample to prospects who respond to an advertisement or mailer.

- Deliver free samples to the target audience through direct marketing or other forms of distribution.

- Include free samples of the promoted product with other products.

Regional pilot trial of a new consumer product

A food manufacturer is launching a new product in an ITV sales region. To support the regional television advertising campaign and retail display programme, the company delivers samples of the product, plus a questionnaire, to all households in the television region using door-to-door distribution. To encourage feedback and capture data for future direct marketing, consumers who return the questionnaire are offered a free recipe book.

Database Action
Use demographic data supplied by the media to plan other channel activities.

Launch of a new training consultancy service

A management consultancy is diversifying into training consultancy. It feels that the best way to market the service is to give a "live demonstration" of the service in action. Existing customers and key prospects are mailed with an offer of a free training audit which enables the prospect to assess the consultancy's skills. The prospect does not have to make any form of financial commitment for the audit, but benefits from an independent assessment of its training activities.

Database Action
Develop a profile for potential users and use this to identify prospects for the promotional offer.

Launching a new book

A publishing company selling its products through direct marketing to an established database launches a new book. Prospects are mailed with sample sections of the book and offered the complete book for a three-week approval period. This offer enables them to assess the potential benefits of the book before buying it.

Database Action
Identify prospects from the database and assess the impact of different offers.

Upgrading computer software
When companies launch a new version of a program, they offer existing customers and users of competitive products a special "upgrade" deal. These prospects pay less than the full price for the latest version of the product.

Database Action
Maintain records of customers and competitive users and measure the uptake of the promotional offer.

PERSUADING CUSTOMERS AND PROSPECTS TO SWITCH BRANDS
The next stage in the marketing process is to persuade prospects to change from their existing choice of product or supplier to the new product or service. It is essential to the success of the following marketing activities:

- Winning business from competitors.

- Launching a new product.

- Launching an existing product into a new market.

- Extending a product range.

- Persuading customers to use a higher value product or service.

Sales promotion can be used to encourage customers and prospects to change and there are a number of potential approaches:

- Free gift or other incentive to change.

- Attractive part exchange deals

- Discounts or money-off coupons on first purchase.

- Match a competitive deal.

- Preferential prices for customers or owners of competitive products who buy a higher value product.

- Offer credit or finance facilities that make it easy for the customer to buy.

Differentiating products with a free gift promotion

A manufacturer of consumer electrical goods wants to win market share from competitors. Pricing and product features are consistent between competitive products and there is little opportunity to differentiate at the point of sale. By offering a free gift, the manufacturer can increase interest in the brand and gain market share.

Database Action
Track the change in sales attributable to the promotional offer.

Catalogue discount vouchers

An industrial company produces a catalogue of replacement parts and accessories available through independent distributors. The distributors also handle competitive parts and accessories, and the company wants to increase its share of distributor business. When it mails the catalogue to customers, it includes a book of vouchers offering discounts on selected high-volume parts and accessories. This helps to encourage initial brand switching and the company uses the voucher information as the basis for a longer term loyalty programme.

Database Action
Monitor the use of the vouchers and record the customer data obtained from the vouchers.

Encouraging customers to buy a higher value service

An independent service company which handles contract maintenance wants to increase the value of its repair contracts and win competitive business. Customers can select bronze, silver or gold options, which provide increasingly higher levels of service. Existing customers who use a lower level of service are offered the higher level at a preferential rate, while users of competitive services are offered silver for the price of bronze or gold for the price of silver as an incentive to take out a contract.

Database Action
Use purchasing history to identify prospects for the different levels of service.

Winning business with finance schemes
Although manufacturers of both consumer and business products have long used finance and credit schemes to win competitive business, the same principles are now being applied in the service sector. A professional firm which offered a range of consultancy, project management and training services identified through research that some of its smaller clients were concerned about high fee levels and so "shopped around" among different consultancies. The firm offered its clients a budget programme. For an agreed monthly fee, the client was able to select services from the firm's portfolio and use them at any time during the 12-month period. So clients who needed to handle a small number of large projects in a short space of time could fund them over the entire period, while clients who needed a number of smaller services at regular intervals knew that their costs would be fixed for the whole year.

Database Action
Use information on purchasing frequency to identify prospects for the promotion.

INCREASING CUSTOMER OR RETAILER LOYALTY
Once customers have switched brands, it is important to build and retain their loyalty. Another sales promotion offer from a competitor could attract those customers away from you again. Sales promotion is one of a number of marketing activities that can be used to manage customer loyalty. Customer and retailer loyalty are essential to the success of the following marketing activities:

● Retaining business against competitors.

● Increasing sales to existing customers.

● Ensuring high levels of repeat purchase.

- Improving the performance of marketing and distribution channels.

- Reducing long-term sales costs.

- Protecting long-term business prospects.

Sales promotion can be used to encourage customers and retailers to continue buying from the same source, and there are a number of potential approaches:

- Volume discounts or money-off coupons for repeat purchase.

- Collector schemes.

- Structured incentives for multiple purchase.

- Competitions linked to purchasing volume.

- Preferential prices for loyal customers.

- Preferential service for loyal customers.

Money-off the next meal

The customer books a meal at a local restaurant. After paying for the meal, the customer receives a book of five vouchers that provides discounts off future meals. Customers who use all five vouchers are then entitled to a complimentary meal for two up to an agreed value. Both customer and restaurant benefit and the highest spending customers receive an additional bonus.

Database Action
Include data capture mechanisms on the vouchers and use the information to plan future promotional offers.

Rewarding regular customers

Collector programmes are becoming increasingly popular in all sectors. Customers receive tokens or points for every purchase and can redeem these for a choice of gifts from a catalogue. For example, a telephone company now offers domestic users with bills over a certain value a collector scheme to reward them for their business. Companies that distribute components and spare parts use collector programmes to encourage higher levels of spending.

Database Action
Capture data to plan future promotional offers.

Moving customers towards regular commitments

A builder's merchant wants to encourage customers to order larger quantities to reduce its delivery costs and wants to increase the number of customers who accept scheduled deliveries on long-term contracts. It offers increased levels of discount for companies which move to the new quantities and even higher levels for customers who place long-term contracts. Customers who place long-term contracts are also given free access to a technical hotline.

Database Action
Track changes in purchasing.

Boosting sales through a customer league table

A manufacturer wants to increase sales to distributors over a four-month period. The company invites 20 key distributors to participate in an incentive programme with eight holiday breaks as the prize. Distributors are grouped in four leagues of five, with the prizes going to the top two in each league. League positions are based on the percentage increase over target sales so that the competition does not favour only large spenders. The competitive element encourages repeat purchase and helps to retain business that might have gone to competitors.

Database Action
Track changes in purchasing levels and frequency resulting from the promotion.

Privileged service and special offers for account customers

Many retailers are using store credit cards to encourage repeat spending. As well as offering the convenience of credit, the retailers also offer special discounts on selected products and mail the account customers with details of forthcoming promotions. The account customers are rewarded for their loyalty with privileged service.

Database Action
Segment the cardholder database and track the response to targeted offers.

Although sales promotion is used primarily to build sales and customer loyalty, it can also make an important contribution to building a brand image. Brand image is essential to the success of the following marketing activities:

● Creating a preference for the product.

● Taking the product into new market sectors.

● Ensuring high levels of customer loyalty.

● Differentiating a product from competitors.

The quality or relevance of sales promotion offers help to reinforce or create an image for the brand and the image should be consistent with other images created by advertising or corporate identity programmes. For example, it would be unsuitable for a professional firm to offer holiday incentives to regular customers, but an invitation to a seminar or a free copy of a management report would be appropriate. Collector schemes can be modified to reflect the brand values of the product or the aspirations of the target audience.

There are a number of potential approaches:

● Gifts that reflect the brand values.

● Targeted collector schemes.

● Structured incentives that reflect the needs of the target audience.

● Competitions linked to advertising themes.

**Building the
image of a
management
consultancy**

A management consultancy wishes to be seen as a leader in the field of human resource development. The consultancy mails customers and prospects with an offer of free invitations to seminars and free copies of a management report on human resource development. The offer reinforces the firm's professionalism and demonstrates its commitment to quality service.

Database Action
Track the response to the offer.

An exclusive club

A national newspaper offers readers a special club card which entitles them to discounts on a wide range of products and services which are carefully selected to reflect the values of the newspaper and the target audience. Club offers are published weekly in the newspaper, encouraging repeat purchase and helping to reinforce brand values over a long period of time.

Database Action
Build a comprehensive reader profile and use the information to make targeted offers.

Busman's holiday

A company supplying vehicle refinishing paints wanted to encourage car repair centres to join a customer club. As an incentive to join, prospects were offered the chance to enter a prize draw to visit an international refinishing exhibition in the US.

Database Action
Measure the effect of the incentive on the uptake of membership.

IMPROVING RETAIL PERFORMANCE

Sales promotion can be used to improve the performance of retail marketing as well as building sales to customers. It is essential to the success of the following retail activities:

● Achieving high levels of distribution.

● Taking the product into new market sectors.

● Ensuring high levels of retailer loyalty.

● Ensuring the right level of point-of-sale impact.

● Reinforcing the impact of other marketing activities.

● Improving standards of customer service through retail outlets.

There are a number of potential approaches:

● Incentives to carry stocks of the product.

- Collector schemes.

- Structured incentives or discounts for increased purchase levels.

- Incentives for using point-of-sale and promotional material.

- Awards for customer service achievements.

Selling-in a new product

A food manufacturer wants to achieve national distribution of a new product range. Successful distribution depends on the co-operation of a number of different national and regional groups, so the company tailors a package of discounts, incentives and marketing support packages to encourage retailers to take initial stocks of the product, with a volume-related discount structure to maintain stock levels for the future.

Database Action
Compare the effect of different elements by varying the offer and measuring response.

Increasing sales of special product groups

An engineering manufacturer identifies five product groups as essential to growth and profitability. To build high levels of repeat business through distributors, the company offers a two-part incentive. Distributors are offered a competitive discount structure, with the opportunity to participate in a league table competition based on purchases over target. The distributors are also given a customer collector scheme which awards points for different levels of purchase of the target products.

Database Action
Measure the change in sales resulting from the incentives.

Improving customer service

Companies which market their products through retail outlets depend on the quality and attitude of local staff to build high levels of customer satisfaction. To encourage local retailers to train their staff and improve levels of customer service, an electrical goods manufacturer operates an incentive programme that rewards participation and achievement in training programmes, as well as good performance in customer surveys. The incentive programme is structured to provide improved discount terms for the outlet, as well as personal awards for high-performing members of staff.

Database Action
Compare the performance of different outlets with the uptake of the promotional offer.

DON'T FORGET!

Sales promotion has been seen as a short-term tactical marketing tool but, combined with database marketing techniques, it can be a powerful weapon in building and retaining customer loyalty. It is essential that any sales promotion programme yields customer information. The information can then be used to develop segmented mailings and track purchasing patterns, while the most sophisticated systems allow cross-selling and the development of long-term customer relationships.

10

operating effective contact strategies

This chapter explains how to plan regular communications with your customers based on an assessment of their information needs. It also describes the importance of carrying out regular communications audits to measure how effectively your contact strategy is working.

identifying communications needs through the database

The database can be used to identify customer information requirements and monitor the effectiveness of contact strategies. This will help to ensure that every contact with the customer is consistent and high quality. It can provide you with the following information:

- The target audience.

- The information each sector has received.

- The follow-up to the communications.

- The customer response.

- Which products and services the customer is interested in.

- How frequently the customer buys the products.

EXAMPLE

Overcoming barriers to a new product

BP Composites developed an advanced composite material that offered designers the advantages of light weight with extremely high strength. The material had been widely used in the aerospace industry but was not yet accepted in general engineering where it was seen as an expensive alternative to traditional materials.

Research among key decision-makers had indicated a possible concern about costs so, to counter possible cost objections, the company concentrated on customer education. It focused the marketing effort not just on the immediate user of the product, but on the other decision-makers who could influence choice.

Targeting all decision-makers

Using information from the database, the company identified the following groups as key decision-makers:

- The designers who specify the material.

- The purchasing managers who needed cost justification.

- The marketing staff and senior executives who would be convinced of the competitive benefits the material could offer their company.

Specialist press information

To refine its prospect information further, the company wrote a series of articles showing how the materials had been used to achieve new performance levels in different engineering sectors. The press programme ran in specialist engineering and design magazines and readers were invited to send for a designer's guide that included the case studies. The response to the articles highlighted potential users in a range of sectors that the company had not considered important.

Designer's guide

This was mailed to designers and engineers in key prospect companies as well as those who responded to the press article. As an incentive to specify the material, designers were offered a special Computer-Aided-Design software package at discount price. The software was pre-programmed with many of the calculations the designers would have to make when using the new material. The company also set up a technical hotline to provide designers with advice and guidance on new projects. The hotline was used to gather information on designers' views of the products and this enabled the company to refine its promotional messages and vary them by sector.

Direct marketing to other decision-makers

Purchasing executives, senior executives and marketing directors in target companies were mailed a management report which outlined the cost-benefits of the new material. The company offered to hold a management workshop for customers to review potential benefits to the company. By measuring the response to this offer, the company was able to assess the level of interest among "indirect influencers". ○

carrying out a communications audit

The BP Composites case study demonstrates the importance of refining a contact strategy through research and feedback. The basic information needed to plan and operate a contact strategy should be established through a communications audit and built into your database. The following example is based on an audit of the planned and current communications between an information systems company and its largest client. It compares the customer's views with those of the supplier and incorporates the customer's views of competitors. The audit compares the actual perceptions against current communications activities and highlights key communications actions needed to achieve the target perception.

The audit should enable you to build a contact strategy on your database that identifies:

- The key decision-makers.

- Their view of the company or products.

- The key messages for each decision-maker.

- The most appropriate media for reaching them.

- A summary of current and planned communications.

You should then use the database to record the communications with each decision-maker and track that against purchasing patterns or image research. In that way the audit can be used as a basis for monitoring changes via the database.

THE AUDIT

Below is a typical management summary of the findings of a communications audit.

The company is setting out to improve the value, market share and quality of its business with this key account, increasing market share from 19 to 25%. To achieve this, the company must secure strategic supplier status and enter a significant collaboration agreement with the customer.

Over the last year the company has improved its image within the key account, but competitors have made further gains. In certain areas the company is highly regarded, but research shows that the customer's senior managers are not aware of the company's current improvement programme. At worst, this means that the company may not be considered for certain major projects and, at best, the company may start at a disadvantage compared with its competitors. The company needs to develop a preference for its products and services, especially in the key areas identified for future business. A strong image development programme will be required to change the attitudes of the customer's senior management team.

The company's current image position could be summarized as follows:

- The company is almost as "visible" as its competitors, but is only rated third in all issues associated with image.

- Contact with the customer at all levels is less than professional. According to the customer, the company does not understand its business and its products, and does not communicate its future strategies.

- There is a legacy of poor reputation which has largely been overcome by increased product reliability, but the image persists in the minds of the customer's senior management team.

- The company is perceived as offering lower quality and lower performance than competitors, and users are less satisfied than competitive users.

- The company is seen as losing ground with important decision-makers.

- The company is identified more clearly than competitors with specific product lines, but is not rated most highly as the potential supplier of those products.

- The company's major weakness is perceived as its narrow product line and lack of expertise in certain areas.

Database Action

- *Record the overall findings of the audit on the database.*

- *Record the findings against individual decision-makers.*

- *Identify the decision-makers where image is worst.*

PLANNING THE STRATEGY

From an image development point of view, there are three major actions needed to ensure future success:

1. The reality of improved performance, reliability and value for money must be sustained and improved.

2. The professionalism of the company's staff, their knowledge of their products and understanding of the customer's needs must be improved. The quality and effectiveness of all contacts with the customer must be improved dramatically.

3. A positive, well-managed and consistent image development programme must be put in place to publicize the company's progress to close the gap between perception and reality and to create a preference for the company by presenting the right messages to the right members of the management team.

Database Action

- *Set communications tasks for each decision-maker.*

- *Identify appropriate communications channels.*

- *Establish desired response levels for ongoing measurement and control.*

CHANGING PERCEPTIONS

The major perceptions which must be created to achieve the business goals are:

- The company is a professional organization which understands the customer's business needs and can meet them with a wide range of high quality products and services.

- The company is technically successful in major projects, developing total solutions and delivering value for money, on time, every time.

- The company is winning share from its competitors.

- The company is an approved and respected strategic supplier with whom it is safe to place business.

- The company is a successful and financially stable company with a sound management team – a good prospective supplier and business partner.

Database Action

- *Record the current levels of awareness of each message.*

- *Measure the changes in levels of awareness.*

THE KEY MESSAGES

Below are a range of key messages that should be targeted at individual decision-makers. The database will indicate which of the messages are important to each decision-maker.

Communicating professionalism

- The company is investing £** in training over the next year.

- The company is organized into market-focused groups to offer the highest standards of service.

- *** staff are dedicated to the customer's business.

- The company is committed to total quality.

- The company has developed a broad product range and a full range of support services.

- The company's products meet international standards.

- The new product development programme is providing innovative new products.

Communicating technical success

- The company has an established reputation for innovation.

- The company's products have been selected for the following demanding applications …

- Customers are saving money by using the company's products.

- The company's products conform to international standards.

- The company has a research and development budget in excess of £*** and has a team of *** highly skilled people dedicated to technical support.

Communicating market success

- The company has been selected to provide products and services to the following customers ...

- The company has recently won a major order worth £** .

- The company has been selected as a strategic supplier to the following customers ...

- The company has gained ** % market share in the last year, while competitors have lost ** % share in the last year.

Communicating strategic supplier status

- The company has been selected as a strategic supplier to the following market-leading customers ...

- The company is collaborating with a major international organization.

- The company meets the following international product and quality standards.

Communicating corporate stability

- The company's annual results show ** % growth in orders, revenue and profits.

- The company is expanding.

- The company is a member of the *** international group.

- The company is the leading European supplier.

> **Database Action**
>
> *The audit has identified the key areas for improving communications performance and it is essential that these messages should be communicated consistently in every form of contact with the customer:*
>
> - *Record details of every contact with the customer.*
>
> - *Measure the effectiveness of each communication in relation to changes in perception.*
>
> - *Calculate the comparative cost of changing attitudes using different communications techniques.*

COMMUNICATIONS STRATEGY

An audit like that helps to identify the key communications tasks. By comparing the tasks with the communications messages that individual customers and prospects are receiving you can plan and monitor a contact strategy using your database.

Here is a simplified example of the way the process might work.

Prospect	ABC Engineering
Contacts	Managing director Technical director Purchasing manager
Perceptions	Managing director – poorly managed company Technical director – innovative, but low quality Purchasing manager – expensive and unreliable on delivery

Action	Managing director – emphasize corporate
	    strengths
	Technical director – communicate quality
	    culture
	Purchasing manager – emphasize value for
	    money

Communications	Managing director – mail corporate brochure
	    coverage in business press
	Technical director – presentation on quality
	Purchasing manager – direct mail on value for
	    money

Response	Managing director – meeting arranged with
	    ABC sales director
	Technical director – requested details of
	    quality programme
	Purchasing manager – request for quotation

Follow-up	Managing director – mail annual report Technical director – offer site visit Purchasing manager – sales call

This simple record could be enhanced to show the response to different types of message, frequency of contact or form of contact.

**DON'T
FORGET!**

Regular communication with customers is essential to the success of long-term marketing success. However, the communications programme must be based on carefully-researched information needs. A communications audit can help you to assess attitudes towards your company and provides the basis for planning a communications strategy. By holding information on the database on the key contacts and their information requirements, you can measure progress towards a purchase or the desired change in perception.

improving local marketing support

This chapter looks at the way companies support branches or retail outlets in their local markets. The key to success is an understanding of the local market and the database can be used to build local market profiles and manage customized local support programmes.

local or national support?

Local marketing programmes are used to provide local outlets with the support they need to build business in their own marketplace. The programmes can operate at two levels:

- The programmes run by suppliers on behalf of all their local outlets.

- The programmes which are provided for outlets to run in their own local markets.

An example of the first programme would be an advertisement running in the specialist engineering or business press. "Use a Brown Engineering-approved distributor for all your components requirements". The local variation would be "All-Components engineering distributor – your local Brown Engineering stockist". Vauxhall's Network Q television commercials have helped to brand every outlet in the network but, at a local level, the outlets would advertise their special offers in the local media.

TRICKS OF THE TRADE

A leading building society ran a recruitment advertisement for a public relations officer to support the local branches in building community relations in their regions. This community relations programme, developed at local level and co-ordinated by head office staff, was to be fully integrated with the society's national television and press advertising campaign which built awareness of the brand.

Marketing programmes such as consumer offers or competitions may "only be available at participating dealerships"; this does not imply that they are customized for local use; it only shows that the programmes are running in limited areas. Price-based promotional programmes are probably the most widely-used local marketing programmes, where local outlets are provided with a standard advertisement format into which they can build their own selection of priced offers together with their own branch information. A further variation of this is the dealer direct mail service where an agency holds a central database of local addresses and sends customized mail-shots to those customers.

Another variation is the promotional kit which provides general guidelines on developing local advertisements and marketing programmes from a series of modular elements. This type of kit contains a guide to planning and operating campaigns plus suggested creative themes and details of any support services available. Some suppliers may have the resources to hire local marketing support staff who provide professional advice and guidance to local outlets.

local database management

The key to the success of local marketing support programmes is detailed knowledge of the local customer base so that the offers and information can be tailored to local marketing programmes. The most efficient way to handle this is to maintain a central database of all local customers and use database management techniques to manage the mailing list. Local outlets are unlikely to have the sophisticated equipment needed to carry out database management operations and the exercise can be carried out more efficiently on a central database.

CONTENTS OF THE DATABASE The database would contain the names and addresses of each outlet's customers, together with variable information such as:

- Purchasing patterns.
- Size of expenditure.
- Type of purchase.
- Number of employees.
- Other variations depending on the type of business.

The database can be utilized to produce targeted mailing lists by describing the product and listing different members of the target audience.

The database can be broken down into categories which correspond to market sectors and the categories can become increasingly specific.

Database information for company offering travel agency training services

Target market

- All travel agencies.
- Agencies belonging to a multiple group.
- Independent agencies.
- Agencies with a turnover in excess of £3 million.
- Agencies with less than 25 staff.
- Sales staff responsible for business travel.
- Sales staff responsible for holiday travel.
- Middle managers with budget responsibility for training.
- Staff with less than one year's travel agency experience.
- Staff with specific qualifications.

Travel agency customers

- Business travellers.
- Leisure travellers.
- Special interest leisure travellers.
- Long-haul travellers.
- Domestic/European business travellers.
- Frequent flyers who cover more than 5000 miles per year.
- First class leisure travellers.

BUILDING THE DATABASE

Information for the database can be gathered from a number of sources, including:

- Local customer sales records.

- Replies to advertisements.

- Responses to special offers or invitations.

- Applications for membership.

- Market research.

The initial database is unlikely to be complete and to provide information in the most suitable format, so companies which wish to benefit from direct marketing run special campaigns to gather appropriate information. For example, an invitation to an open evening or a prize draw would require customers to provide information that is essential for the database.

Local outlets can be given guidelines on the way to build and maintain their own records so that they provide suitable input to the database. The database is then built to meet local marketing objectives. By managing the process centrally and working in close conjunction with local outlets, suppliers can ensure that their local outlets enjoy a professional quality direct marketing service that is precisely tailored to their local market.

national support programmes

A national support programme is a visible demonstration that the supplier is helping local outlets to market their services. When a supplier wants to recruit new franchisees or build up a local network, part of the promise is that the supplier will help the local outlet to build business.

A national support programme can help to build a strong brand identity for a network of branches and assure customers that they will receive a high standard of service wherever they see the sign. An approach like this is important when the network consists of a fragmented group of independent branches which have no cohesive identity. The national programme helps to build them into a single unit and enables them to benefit from large national advertising campaigns. In the example below, the advertiser runs a national campaign to generate database information for local outlets.

EXAMPLE

Gucci Timepieces

Gucci Timepieces, a member of the world-famous Gucci group which produces high quality leather goods, wanted to build a strong UK distributor network and to make consumers aware that they could buy Gucci around the country and get first-class service. Its local support programme included a distributor information pack which described the Gucci philosophy, explained the requirements of the Gucci franchise and outlined the support that Gucci would give to the distributor. To launch the brand, Gucci ran a national advertising campaign in prestige publications and enclosed a reply coupon encouraging prospects to write for the name of their local distributor. The prospects were sent the name of the distributor and were also given a leaflet explaining the standard of service they should expect from the distributor. The distributors were provided with a wide range of merchandising material so that they could brand their own outlets. As part of the continuing programme of national support, Gucci ran major national advertising campaigns during the peak gift buying seasons when sales were at their highest levels. Gucci's national campaigns were raising awareness of its national network and helping to build its business. ○

Other suppliers have tried to build the reputation of their local outlets with a phrase like, "the sign of a good ..." which explains the benefits of dealing with a particular retail outlet. Advertising is used as part of a long-term strategic marketing programme to build awareness and confidence in the local network, but a national support campaign contains more than just advertising.

STRATEGIC PROMOTION

National promotional campaigns are used to attract customers for short or long periods. A national promotional campaign like the Esso Tiger Tokens is fully integrated with the national advertising campaign which stresses the quality of the petrol and the broad range of products and services available from an Esso outlet.

Esso Tiger Tokens

EXAMPLE

Esso Tiger Tokens, a programme which has now become the Esso Collection, is both tactical and strategic. Its tactical value is that it can encourage customers to switch between brands to obtain free gifts and it takes the emphasis away from price difference. But, in the long term, it is a valuable strategic branding programme. The Esso Collection includes a choice of quality merchandise presented in a well-produced "lifestyle" catalogue, and the high product values encourage brand loyalty by ensuring that customers keep buying Esso petrol to achieve their gifts. ○

Token collectors provide a valuable source of data for future direct marketing activities and many companies are now looking more closely at the value of the data they can obtain. There is an increasing trend towards using smart cards to allow consumers to "accumulate" points and supply useful data on purchasing habits through local outlets. This information can be used by the database to measure the effectiveness of different types of local or regional promotion and compare the performance of local outlets during promotional periods.

mandatory programmes

While national support programmes have benefits for both supplier and local outlet, there are a number of programmes that are crucial to achieving the right standards of customer service. These programmes give the supplier a degree of control over critical local operations. The database is used to record details of the dealerships who are participating and to monitor their performance against regional and national standards. By integrating the results from customer satisfaction surveys, the database can provide valuable information for controlling the programme.

EXAMPLE

Customer satisfaction programmes

When Ford introduced customer satisfaction programmes such as Courtesy Car, it was essential that every dealership participated because the programmes are designed to increase service business by improving customer convenience. Although the dealers have discretion in the way they operate the programme at local level, it is vital that every dealership offers the service because it is an integral part of the customer care programme. ○

---

participation in other programmes

Not all support programmes are mandatory. By offering local outlets a choice of programmes, suppliers can tailor their marketing to suit local market conditions. The programmes might include:

- Local advertising.
- Direct mail.
- Product literature.
- Display material.
- Merchandising material.
- Competitions.
- Special offers.

- Public relations support.

- Community activities.

The database can be used to measure how effectively the individual programmes are used by the outlets. It can provide information on:

- The use of support materials by outlet.

- The cost of local marketing activities.

- The contribution of the campaigns to sales performance.

- Comparative performance by different outlets.

- The effectiveness of different local media.

To improve flexibility, suppliers produce a guide to support programmes which enables the local outlet to select programmes that allow them to develop their own promotional strategies. The guides should:

- Explain the scope and benefits of individual programmes.

- Describe the support material available to operate the programme.

- Explain how to order support material.

- Provide guidelines on running the programmes.

WATCH OUT!

Many suppliers have tried to avoid serious levels of support by providing an ad-hoc collection of support material. This is not the same as providing business support and it should not be used as a substitute for serious planning.

tailoring programmes

The value of mandatory national support campaigns is that they minimize the cost of support management by providing standard programmes with the minimum of extra effort. However, the programmes may offer limited benefit and may build the long-term branding without being responsive to short-term sales requirements.

The database allows support programmes to be tailored to the needs
of local markets and monitored to ensure that they are operating effectively.

modular support programmes

In the programme described below, database information on competitive activity was crucial to the success of the programme. "Selling Service" was designed to help franchised local dealers compete effectively
against independent service operations and therefore a pricing strategy
that reflected local conditions was essential. Continuous pricing
research was integrated with the database to provide local information.

EXAMPLE

The Ford Selling Service Programme

The Ford "Selling Service" Programme was designed as a modular kit
which could be easily tailored to local conditions. The kit was in the
form of an "action pack" which contained all the material dealers
needed to operate a wide range of business and promotional programmes. To
ensure that the programme operated effectively, the field salesforce worked with
dealers to analyze the local market and select the programmes that were most
appropriate. The dealers also had access to an agency service which provided them
with professional support for research, advertising planning and direct marketing as
well as supplying a range of customized advertisements and direct mail-shots. The
support programme was also integrated with a local training initiative which
improved the skills of distributor staff. All the ingredients were there to provide a
fully-integrated business development programme. ○

TAILORING THE PROGRAMME THROUGH RESEARCH

The programme was developed to help dealers regain the service business they were losing to independents and chains such as Halfords. Research carried out before the programme was launched identified customers' key concerns over the service they received from franchised dealers and analyzed the reasons they preferred other forms of service. This research provided a basis for developing a series of dealership standards and a range of service offers which were right for the market. Dealers were also encouraged to carry out research in their own territories to identify the local competition and their own potential customer base. Priced offers were an essential element of the dealer offer and a research agency was commissioned to carry out nationwide price surveys on a wide range of products and service offers and to work with distributors to develop local pricing strategies.

MANDATORY AND OPTIONAL MODULES

Part of the programme was mandatory to ensure that dealers were able to provide the right standards of service, while the other modules allowed them to attack different sectors of the market. The mandatory modules were based on a series of customer focus standards and the dealers were given guidelines on how to achieve them.

The database was key to the success of the other modules in the programme. Local dealers analyzed their own market profiles to highlight sectors where they wanted to improve performance.

A range of other modules provided dealers with plans, programmes and support material to develop effective marketing strategies for different market sectors. For example, it covered selling service to business users, women, the used car market and high profile motorists. It also provided detailed plans for setting up customer events such as a women's workshop or for establishing a "quickfit" type operation for selling fast-moving exhausts, tyres or batteries in competition with independent specialists. Finally, the guide included a series of priced offer advertisements and seasonal promotions which could be customized with the dealer's name, address and price offers.

To put the programme into operation, dealers were asked to prepare a business plan and marketing strategy, together with an allocation of budget based on current and forecast turnover. Ford would then agree its contribution to the programme and the dealer launched the programme. The details and costs of individual dealer programmes were logged on the database and monitored.

<table>
<tr><td>

**BUSINESS
DEVELOPMENT
OPTIONS**

</td><td>

A similar modular approach was taken by the German car paint manufacturer, Spies Hecker, which sold a wide range of products to franchised and independent bodyshops. Although distributors had received extensive marketing support in the past, it was apparent that marketing support alone would not be sufficient to help the bodyshops improve their performance. The bodyshop was an important part of the entire car dealership operation and made a significant and growing contribution to overall turnover and profit. With the increasing levels of competition and the higher levels of investment needed to provide a quality service, it was important that the bodyshop ran an efficient business operation. Spies Hecker worked closely with the local distributor to provide the right level of support to the bodyshop.

</td></tr>
<tr><td>

**THE SUPPORT
DATABASE**

</td><td>

A support database was developed to build a profile of the business support needs of individual outlets.

</td></tr>
</table>

- The first part of the programme was a bodyshop self-analysis which enables the bodyshop manager to analyze his current business and future prospects in a logical way and formulate plans based on that. The guide leads the bodyshop manager through a series of questions relating to:

  - the type of customers

  - prospects

  - competition

  - business conditions.

  The bodyshop can then build up a clear picture of its customer base and competitive activity.

- The next stage is to analyze strengths and weaknesses as a basis for building a bodyshop action plan. The strengths and weaknesses section asks bodyshops questions about the way they handle different aspects of their business. The analysis also provides information that can be used to build up copy for advertisements and direct mail.

- When the bodyshop staff have completed their self-analysis, they put together a business plan which is reviewed in conjunction with the local distributor and the Spies Hecker sales representative. The business plan incorporates the actions they will take together with their advertising and marketing proposals.

Spies Hecker is then in a position to provide help at a number of levels. The "Partners in Profit" programme incorporates a number of different modules to improve the business and an increasing number are supplied on software for use on personal computers. By providing management and accounting packages, it can ensure that the bodyshop improves its financial performance and control, throughput, productivity and workshop loading.

Financial performance depends on good control and the business packages ensure that bodyshops understand every aspect of their financial performance and provide a competitively-priced and profitable service to customers. The "Partners in Profit" programme also includes technical advisory and planning services to ensure that bodyshops are able to take advantage of the latest refinishing techniques.

The value of this programme to Spies Hecker is that it encourages and supports a programme of self development. Distributors are able to take advantage of the modular package and work closely with their customers to tailor the programme to their requirements. The elements of the programme are planned and produced centrally and controlled via the central database, but the programme operates independently at local level.

local direct marketing

The essence of an effective local support programme is that local outlets understand their customers' needs and provide a level of service that is tailored to that market. In terms of customer satisfaction, the most powerful medium available to companies is direct marketing.

CUSTOMIZING LOCAL COMMUNICATIONS

When ICL introduced the Customer Reception Centre, a single point of contact for customers throughout the country, it realized that branches would be reluctant to lose day-to-day contact with their local customers, so it balanced this with a programme of regular customer care visits which enabled the branch to take a proactive role in communications with customers.

The first stage in the process was a direct mail-shot which included a brochure on the benefits of the new central Customer Reception Centre, together with a personalized letter from the local branch manager explaining the changing and more positive role of the branch. The brochure itself was customized with a map showing the location of the branch and the letter was addressed to customers individually. A mailing like this had the benefit of centralized design and production to ensure quality and consistency, but it bore the name of the local outlet to ensure the right level of contact.

A more conventional use of direct marketing is the specific offer to customers of a local outlet. Here local customer information is maintained on a central database and the mailings are issued centrally and tracked to assess comparative regional and local performance.

EXAMPLE

Spring Motoring Check

The Spring Motoring Check is one of a range of seasonal offers made by car dealers to build local service business. Customers are offered a free safety check, plus a report on any service or maintenance needed, together with an estimate. Each dealership nominates its own prices or offers within overall guidelines and is able to make a special seasonal gift offer as an added incentive. The mail-shots are produced centrally and overprinted with the detailed local information before central distribution to produce a tailored local offer. ○

**TRICKS OF
THE TRADE**

British Airways' Speedwing Training programme relies on carefully targeted direct mail exercises to provide each of the local travel agents in the network with customized training programmes. The training agency develops a database with all the information on local skills and business requirements, and then mails details of individual training programmes to each travel agent. The travel agent only receives relevant information and does not have to sift through unwanted information.

SUPPORTING SECTOR MARKETING

Although that programme is designed to improve relationships between a company and its agents, the same technique can be used to support travel agents marketing to their customers. Galileo, a company owned by a group of international airlines, provides computerized information and reservation systems to travel agents. Using the Galileo system, a travel agent can offer customers a fast efficient service that is vital to winning and retaining business. To help travel agents communicate the benefits to their customers, Galileo used its own customer database to develop a series of mailings aimed at different sectors of the market such as business travellers, package holiday customers and special interest holidays. A series of letters and offers is available to the travel agents for customization on their own personal computer systems and the letters have identified variables for modification by the travel agent.

The programme can be easily modified to suit the individual travel agent's own customer profile. If, for example, the agent handles a high level of business travel and the agent has information on the travelling patterns of its customers, it could offer special deals on car hire, hotels and entertainment for the travellers' regular destinations. It could also ensure that individual business travellers took full advantage of the "frequent flyer" offers made by many of their major airlines.

EXAMPLE

Air UK

Air UK, an independent airline based at Stansted, provided its travel agents with a customized mailing service based on knowledge of business travel destinations. It had identified, through analysis of customer patterns, that a high level of business was coming from companies in financial engineering and the oil business using regional airports to fly staff to and from London via Stansted. The company ran a series of advertisements in local newspapers within the catchment areas of the regional airports to build the perception of Air UK and Stansted as the most efficient way to meet domestic and regional travel, and then worked in conjunction with local travel agents to develop a direct marketing programme aimed at the most important market sectors.

The travel agents identified the companies within their regions which fitted the travelling profile – head office or branch in the region and other branches or head office in London or one of the regional airports. They mailed these companies with introductory information on the Air UK service and offered to carry out an analysis of their UK travel requirements. The agent then operated a regular mailing programme which included special offers for regular travellers, together with personalized gifts. This direct marketing was integrated with the national and regional advertising campaign and demonstrates the value of co-operation between an operator and agents. ○

customized advertising service

Local or regional advertising campaigns can be customized to suit the needs of the local market. Support can be delivered in a number of forms:

- Funds to enable local outlets to produce and run their own advertisements.

- Contributions to the cost of joint supplier/local outlet advertisements.

- Contributions to the cost of advertisements run by regional groups of outlets.

- Production of national support advertisements which incorporate local information and which are run on a regional basis.

- Support for advertisements run in conjunction with regional radio or television stations.

Providing this type of support requires a considerable degree of programme management and a database that records and monitors the local advertising activities is essential. The database can be used to track:

- The type of support material supplied.

- The response to different campaign elements.

- Expenditure against budget.

- Expenditure by region.

- Campaign results.

FUNDING OPTIONS

The level of support depends on the funds available for local support and the outlet's own budget. For example, many independent outlets have substantial advertising budgets of their own and utilize the suppliers' budgets to supplement their own or to run specific campaigns. Other smaller outlets or franchised outlets without their own budgets rely entirely on the supplier's contribution to run local campaigns. Because of this, the question of financial support is usually subject to negotiation. The database allows you to record and monitor expenditure against budget.

SUPPLYING ADVERTISING MATERIAL

The more practical forms of support – complete advertisements, logos, artwork, photographs – can be supplied for inclusion in the outlet's own local campaigns. The supplier is likely to be more concerned about the consistency of local advertisements than the local outlet, and should issue clear guidelines on the use of different elements of corporate identity. Many suppliers provide advertising standard manuals which give examples of layouts for different sizes of advertisements, explain the position and size of the company name and logo, list the typefaces to use and include sample advertisements for guidance.

The database can be used to hold local information for customizing advertisements or mail-shots and to track usage of the material.

CENTRALIZED ADVERTISING SERVICES

Alternatively, the supplier can offer local outlets a central advertising service. This support policy enables suppliers to offer local outlets consistent professional advertisement standards, with local information such as name and address, map, priced offers, product variations and special offers incorporated. The local outlet benefits from national advertising and strong branding, but they have advertisements that suit the local market.

The database can be used to assess the effectiveness of different local media and the impact of different levels of local expenditure.

ADVERTISING IN TEST MARKETS

Local advertising support can also be used in test markets. Here, the company can vary price, product or promotional support to evaluate the effect of different programmes. In consumer goods marketing, many suppliers utilize the marketing services offered by regional television, press or radio. The media provide the demographic and market information on their region and the supplier can then develop a suitable local campaign. The media will also provide support in the form of merchandising and contract research into the needs of the local market. The supplier places advertisements in the media and is able to evaluate the effectiveness of the campaign.

The database is used to compare the results of different media, different levels of expenditure and the impact of other promotional activities.

DON'T FORGET!

The database allows you to identify local marketing requirements and produce customized support material that reflects local market conditions. The database is also crucial to managing and measuring local support programmes.

12

opening new marketing channels

This chapter looks at the ways in which database marketing can support new marketing channels such as direct sales and direct response advertising. It also looks at the potential of new media and the role of the database in using them.

the direct route

Increasingly companies in sectors such as financial services and computers are adopting a "direct" approach and selling directly to customers rather than through retailers or distributors.

EXAMPLE

First Direct

When First Direct introduced round the clock telephone banking, it was a breakthrough in customer service. Customers enjoy a personal service whenever they choose to do business and they can carry out transactions without visiting a branch. First Direct utilized the power of database information and communications to improve personal service beyond what was available from the rest of the high street banking system. As well as improving customer service, it was also opening profitable new marketing channels. ○

Technology had been used to automate many traditional banking processes and the result had been a reduction in personal contact and a loss of identity. Automatic tellers, direct debits and other forms of automation meant that customers no longer needed to visit their branch. Although that might have increased efficiency and allowed the banks to improve their productivity and reduce costs, it meant that they had lost contact with their customers.

There is a parallel in the insurance business where companies had traditionally maintained a field force of collectors and agents calling on households. Direct debits and other forms of automated payment enabled the insurance company to reduce its overheads but lose vital contact. First Direct's use of technology was innovative in the finance sector. Banks and building societies had invested heavily in information technology (IT) as a means of improving productivity. At one level, IT was seen as a way of freeing staff to deal with customers; there was a clear distinction between front and back office duties and IT was seen as a way of dealing with the back office issues. This enabled banks and building societies to open up the traditional counter area to give staff and customers the chance to meet in a more personal environment. Cash dispensers and other automated processes helped customers deal with routine transactions and freed the counter staff to deal with customer queries, loans and other services. This trend is in line with the long-term business strategy of offering customers a wider portfolio of financial services, including insurance, mortgages, investment advice, stocks and shares, and financial advice with the aim of building customers for life.

By providing customers with cash dispensers, increased levels of direct debiting and other facilities for automated transactions, customers had less reason for visiting a branch, and contact was reduced rather than increased. Many customers felt that they were simply account numbers and that personal service was a thing of the past. First Direct focused clearly on what it saw were the customers' real needs – a personal service at a convenient time for the customer, with a high degree of flexibility. The concept was simple – 24-hour banking by telephone. A customer rings up at any time and is able to carry out a wide range of transactions over the telephone. Far from being an impersonal telephone service, the First Direct contact was perceived as a friendly and personal service where the customer was treated as an individual, rather than a number.

ROLE OF THE DATABASE

The key to effective "direct" sales activities is the database. At minimum it should contain the following information:

- Name.
- Address.
- Account number.
- Purchase history.
- Preferences/special requirements.
- Products and services bought .
- Frequency of purchase.
- Contact history.

Once the database is established it can be used for the following activities:

- Identifying likely purchasing patterns.

- Analysing customer information as a means of cross-selling other products and services.

- Assessing the effectiveness of marketing programmes

The database enables the telephone staff to handle incoming callers efficiently and identify opportunities for marketing other services. For example, the database can identify prospects for services such as life assurance, services or loans. When a customer calls, the screen prompts the operator to mention any relevant products. The customer's response is logged and the system then prompts follow-up action such as mailing further information or offering a quotation. This process can then be tracked until the prospect buys the product.

applying the direct approach

The "direct" approach is now being found in a number of other markets and it can be used to meet different scenarios where:

- Customers carry out specific transactions which do not depend on specialist skills.

- Computers provide all the customer information necessary to carry out transactions. Customer details are held on personal computer and can be accessed by any member of the telephone team.

- The customer sees convenience as an important aspect of the service and this convenience is not available through other forms of service delivery. In this case, customers would have to visit a branch, they may not have time or the location could be difficult.

- The service can be positioned as prompt, flexible and personal and can be tailored to the needs of individual customers.

- Quality of personal service is seen as more important than location.

- People and resources can be concentrated in specific areas, rather than scattered around a branch network.

- The service does not have to be located in a particular area and it does not have to be situated near the mechanism for delivering the service; for example, telephone banking does not require a high street location.

- The service can be branded although it has no physical existence for the customer. This runs contrary to the traditional feeling of the banks that oak panel and marble were essential to the image of stability they wished to convey.

DON'T FORGET!

In setting up a service like this, there are a number of important considerations:

- ○ *Deliver a quality service to the customer.*

- ○ *Offer the customer maximum convenience.*

- ○ *Provide customers with a prompt, flexible service.*

- ○ *Utilize the power and flexibility of the database and the telephone to deliver a personal service.*

- ○ *Compete effectively with traditional methods of service delivery.*

Direct Line Insurance

EXAMPLE

Direct Line Insurance carved out a profitable niche in the car insurance market by offering customers a highly efficient telesales and claims handling operation. Rather than contact a broker or a traditional insurance company direct the customer was able to benefit from a professional, no-frills operation. By reducing its overheads and not having to support a salesforce or a branch network, the company was able to offer an extremely competitive service. When prospects called, their enquiry was handled by trained sales staff who worked through a planned sequence of questions to ensure the customer received an accurate quote. The quote was handled on computer and was immediate. If the customer accepted the quote, the policy was immediately put into effect and no further action was needed. Claims were handled in the same straightforward way. The customer phoned in, described the incident and the claim would be dealt with rapidly. This standard of service enabled Direct Line to post good profits and set a standard that other insurance companies tried to follow. ○

The Direct Line database enabled telesales staff to streamline the process of handling enquiries by providing prompts for information. The company is now using its customer database to market a range of related financial services products, using the same customer proposition of speedy customer service.

benefits of the direct approach

Putting the programme into operation provided important benefits for both client and service provider. Customers had a service that was focused on their needs:

- The service provided the highest levels of convenience and flexibility.

- Customers could deal with their financial affairs in the most convenient way.

- They were able to have access to a personal adviser who could deal with any aspect of their financial affairs.

- Financial affairs could be handled at times that were convenient to the customer.

- Customers could make transactions and get an immediate picture of their situation.

The benefits to the provider were equally important:

- They were able to reach a new market which was looking for a specific type of service.

- They could take advantage of technology to deliver a highly-efficient service.

- They could concentrate their resources by utilizing technology to deliver a consistent nationwide service to every customer.

- The investment in technology and communications set up strong entry barriers that deterred competition.

marketing on the Internet

The Internet is beginning to attract attention as a marketing channel and advertising medium. So far, only a comparatively small number of advertisers have experimented with the medium, but an increasing number of companies are investigating it and the Internet is acquiring a network of suppliers who can provide advice and guidance.:

- Worldwide users approximately 7.9 million.

- 200,000 UK users with full Internet access.

- 66% of users are males aged 18–35.

- 60–80% of users are college educated.

- 50–60% of users are white collar workers.

- 35% earned over £25,000 per year.

EARLY MARKETERS

Barclaycard

Barclaycard Netlink is an electronic magazine. Users were offered monthly Internet-related prizes. 15,000 users accessed the magazine in the first two weeks and 70 users requested Barclaycard application forms in the same period.

American Express

American Express offered customers online access to account information, together with travel-related information on a wide range of destinations. 70,000 card holders enrolled for the service and 10,000 new card applications were generated.

Daily Telegraph

The Daily Telegraph introduced an online newspaper, The Electronic Telegraph. It attracted 90,000 subscribers and 80,000 pages a day were requested. The majority of "readers" were under 40 and most read it at work. The Telegraph received an increasing demand for advertisements in areas such as cars, travel and appointments.

Price Jamieson Recruitment Consultants

Price Jamieson offers news of management appointments over the Internet and sees this as a valuable way of positioning itself as a leading edge consultancy.

THE MARKETING OPPORTUNITIES

The marketing opportunities are still being established, but there is an emerging pattern: The "World-wide web" is seen as the primary medium for marketers. This is a collection of Internet "sites" linked by hypertext. Users can set up their own "sites" or rent them from an agency. A site is the equivalent of a shop window and could take a number of forms:

- Electronic catalogues giving product information.

- Price lists.

- Advertisements.

- Response mechanisms and order forms.

- Multimedia product demonstrations.

Smaller advertisers can take "pages" in specialist areas of the Internet. If a user is accessing related information, the advertisement page is available for browsing.

the Internet and database marketing

The indications are that the Internet will prove to be a suitable medium for relationship marketing. The database will play an important role in profiling prospects and "sites" and selecting the most appropriate Internet channels. A number of the early Internet users, such as The Electronic Telegraph, have already established their own electronic database and provide users with electronic access. They are therefore able to monitor usage levels and track purchasing patterns against different types of advertisement.

The Internet is an interactive medium, advertisers should therefore seek to obtain a response. Marketers should not assume the Internet is a mass medium, despite the growing number of users. The medium is controlled by the user, ie it is easy to ignore advertisements; early research indicates that users may seek out appropriate information supplied by advertisers provided it offers real value.

Marketing material must therefore offer users a tangible benefit. Examples include prizes, offers of reduced cost access to other Internet services or unique services only available on the Internet. Material must be carefully prepared to take advantage of the medium. Proprietary software packages are available for advertisers to design their own pages and agency services are available.

The Internet allows use of more sophisticated multi-media techniques, provided the medium is appropriate and the advertiser has the budget. Customer convenience is essential. The Internet offers users 24-hour access so round-the-clock online ordering is possible.

A response mechanism is essential so that users can obtain further information. Observers believe the Internet is more suitable for building relationships than traditional advertising.

**SUITABLE
PRODUCTS AND
SERVICES**

Among the early users of the Internet are companies which rely on communicating large amounts of updatable information. These include:

- Financial services companies.

- Travel-related companies

- Information publishers, including newspapers.

- Companies handling enquiries/reservations.

- Recruitment consultancies.

DON'T FORGET!

Database marketing enables you to support and evaluate new marketing channels. The "direct" route is increasingly used in a variety of markets and its success is based on the use of a customer database to enhance customer handling and support cross-selling. Emerging media such as the Internet offer new opportunities for relationship marketing and will take database marketing a stage further.

index